To Kabl...

Ho...

to...

au...

Ingrid

PROUST

A BEGINNER'S GUIDE

INGRID WASSENAAR

Series Editors
Rob Abbott & Charlie Bell
Drawings
Steve Coots

Hodder & Stoughton

A MEMBER OF THE HODDER HEADLINE GROUP

Orders: please contact Bookpoint Ltd, 39 Milton Park, Abingdon, Oxon OX14 4TD. Telephone: (44) 01235 827720, Fax: (44) 01235 400454. Lines are open from 9.00–6.00, Monday to Saturday, with a 24-hour message answering service. Email address: orders@bookpoint.co.uk

British Library Cataloguing in Publication Data
A catalogue record for this title is available from The British Library

ISBN 0 340 78907 7

First published 2000
Impression number   10 9 8 7 6 5 4 3 2 1
Year   2005 2004 2003 2002 2001

Copyright © 2000 Ingrid Wassenaar
Series editors Rob Abbott and Charlie Bell

Illustrations by Steve Coots
Typeset by Transet Limited, Coventry, England.
Printed in Great Britain for Hodder & Stoughton Educational, a division of Hodder Headline Plc, 338 Euston Road, London NW1 3BH by Cox & Wyman, Reading, Berks

CONTENTS

Contents

Introduction

HOW TO USE THIS BOOK

The *Beginner's Guide* series aims to introduce readers to the major writers of the past 500 years. It is assumed that readers will begin with little or no knowledge and will want to go on to explore the writer in other ways.

Begin reading Proust

This book is a companion guide to Proust's major works: it is not a substitute for reading the works themselves. The author, Ingrid Wassenaar, suggests that the best way to understand Proust is to read him. This *Beginner's Guide* is divided into sections. After considering how to approach Proust's work and a chronology and brief biography, Ingrid goes on to explore *A la recherche du temps perdu* and its themes before examining some critical approaches to the author. Her technique is to deal with themes and content as they arise, putting them into the context of the novel. The survey finishes with suggestions for reading and possible areas of further study.

HOW TO APPROACH UNFAMILIAR OR DIFFICULT TEXTS

Coming across a new writer may seem daunting, but do not be put off. The trick is to persevere. Much good writing is multi-layered and complex. It is precisely this diversity and complexity which makes literature rewarding and exhilarating.

Literature often needs to be read more than once, and in different ways. These ways can include: a leisurely and superficial reading to get the main ideas and narrative; a slower more detailed reading focusing on the nuances of the text, concentrating on what appear to be key passages; and reading in a random way, moving back and forth through the text to examine such things as themes, or narrative or characterisation. Each reader has their own approach but undoubtedly the best way to extract the most from a text is to read it several times.

In complex texts it may be necessary to read in short sections. Sometimes the only way to get by is to skip through the text, going back over it later. When it comes to tackling difficult words or concepts it is often enough to guess in context on the first reading, making a more detailed study using a dictionary or book of critical concepts on later reading. If you prefer to look up unusual words as you go along, be careful that you do not disrupt the flow of the text and your concentration.

VOCABULARY

You will see that KEY TERMS and unfamiliar words are set in **bold** text. These words are defined and explained in the GLOSSARY to be found at the back of the book. In order to help you further we have also summarised each section in our SUMMARIES.

You can read this introductory guide in its entirety, or dip in wherever suits you. You can read it in any order. It is a tool to help you appreciate a key figure in literature. We hope you enjoy reading it and find it useful.

✳ ✳ ✳ ✳ *SUMMARY* ✳ ✳ ✳ ✳

To maximise the use of this book:

- Read the author's work.

- Read it several times in different ways.

- Be open to innovative or unusual forms of writing.

- Persevere.

ROB ABBOTT AND CHARLIE BELL
SERIES EDITORS

Why read *A la recherche du temps perdu* today?

Marcel Proust wrote one of the world's longest, most important, and least well-known novels, *A la recherche du temps perdu*. Many people, asked who Proust was and what he wrote, however, might reply, 'he was a snob and a dilettante who wrote a really long novel about *madeleine* cakes'. This Beginner's Guide is going to demystify Proust's novel.

* It will take you through the whole of *A la recherche du temps perdu*.
* It will outline the big ideas that Proust had.
* Finally it will introduce some current approaches to reading Proust (as if the novel itself were not enough).

The most important thing this book has to say is that you should put it down and go and read *A la recherche* instead.

WHY IS PROUST RELEVANT?

* Proust is a vital figure in European culture. He is a writer whose range of subject matter, perception, and powers of analysis put him on a par with Ovid, Shakespeare, Dante, Goethe. He is undoubtedly one of Western literature's greats.

* *A la recherche* is an early twentieth-century novel. Proust wrote at a time of major scientific, artistic and political transformation. Our own technology-intensive and individualistic epoch is deeply unsettling. Its central issues have their roots in the way Europe was changing at the end of the nineteenth century. Proust made a very particular contribution to this major shift in attitudes. It was a book about how **subjectivity** works.

> **KEYWORD**
>
> Subjectivity individual perspective on the world; personal preferences and desires, based on formative early influences.

* Proust researched the *dangers* of self-analysis. He wrote about deeply held anxieties, and came up with theories about why these anxieties become so entrenched. These theories do not always flatter our sensibilities.

* He can be equated with Einstein, Freud or Marx, in that his way of analysing the nature of time and memory is just as sustained and experimental as the way the formulators of relativity, the unconscious, and Communism worked.

* He was in effect a scientist of literature, a risk-taking experimentalist. He is engrossed with analysing brain activity, sexuality, language, social exclusion, the way we negotiate time, and why we care at all about making works of art.

* He believed that we understand and learn through error not through success. He also believed that we learn best through the analysis of minute details. Proust was a writer who couldn't stop remodelling the same thing until he felt he had got to the bottom of it. *A la recherche* can be seen as a fantastically well-supplied laboratory and logbook of his experiments.

* He was a technical innovator. First-person confessional fiction owes a huge debt to Proust. He also plays around with time. Conventionally, we pretend that time moves in a straight line, even though we do not experience time like this. Proust does not write in a straightforward linear way, but hops backwards and forwards, and repeats events from different points of view. We can understand flashback and multiple perspectives in films and novels easily now. Proust is one of the people who accustomed us to representing reality in this unstable way.

PROUST AND THE TECHNOLOGICAL REVOLUTION

Most Western democracies are concerned today with a massive social, political and economic restructuring process. Modern technology enables us to work alone, far from each other, and at the same time generates the illusion that we are closely connected. We expect instant (and complete) communication and we find it almost incomprehensible that communication might need to take place over time, or not be available to everyone all at the same time.

Proust was writing as this technological revolution began. Cinema developed during his lifetime. The telephone was in more widespread use. Photography was enabling everyone to record themselves and their lives, instantly and repeatedly. People could fly in aeroplanes. Proust tried to monitor the effects of increased and accelerated mobility and the multiplying opportunities for all kinds of connections (economic, sexual, linguistic, photographic).

He found himself in a twentieth century at war with itself, frantically mixing up the class system, and discovering invisible particles. It was giving women positions of power, giving up on organized religion, transmitting vast amounts of information, re-evaluating sexuality, and unable to decide whether art was a decorative commodity for the very rich or a way of reflecting on the human condition. Proust wanted to map mobility.

2 Approaching Proust's work

WHERE SHOULD I BEGIN?

Proust's major work is a long novel called *A la recherche du temps perdu*. There are excellent translations, and there are parts of the novel that stand alone. Look at the section *Where Next?* for guidance on which editions to look for.

A la recherche is a single, continuous novel, although it is so long that it has to be published in separate volumes. It runs to approximately 3,000 pages.

The opening section of *A la recherche* is called *Du côté de chez Swann* (*Swann's Way*). This section itself falls into three parts. The first two, *Combray*, and *Un Amour de Swann* (*Swann in Love*) are the most famous sections in the novel, apart from the very end section, *Le temps retrouvé* (*Time Regained*). *Combray* is the name of the village where the narrator of the novel spends his childhood. Swann is the name of an important character in *A la recherche*.

The other sections of the novel are:

* *A l'ombre des jeunes filles en fleurs* (literally, *In the Shade of Blossoming Girls*)

* *Le Côté de Guermantes* (roughly, *Taking The Guermantes Way*)

* *Sodome et Gomorrhe* (as it sounds!)

* *La Prisonnière* (*The Prisoner* – but it is important to realize that this prisoner is *female*)

* *Albertine disparue* (literally *Albertine Disappeared*. *Disparue* means gone, lost, vanished. In French, it is also a euphemism for 'dead')

* *Le temps retrouvé* (literally *Time Regained*).

IS PROUST A DIFFICULT WRITER?

The answer is both yes and no. Proust wrote in a very unusual style, with long sentences that unfold into seemingly endless clauses. He used a rich vocabulary, and a hallmark of his style is his use of **metaphor**.

A question often asked about *A la recherche* is whether it is fiction or an autobiography. This can be cleared up immediately. It is a work of fiction. Proust wrote in the first person and this is one clear source of confusion. The other is that he used material from his life which he *reworked* and *transformed* into fiction. Every writer does this, and Proust was telling us a great deal about how writers create by 'showing

KEYWORD

Metaphor a figure of speech in which one thing is described in terms of another. (But see the section on Proust's use of metaphor in the chapter entitled 'Proust's Major Themes and Ideas').

his working' as he does. The most famous example of 'showing the working' is that the first person narrator is named several times in the novel – and his name is the same as the novel's author: Marcel.

Proust is a difficult writer to the extent that many of his insights are painful, and because there are so many of them. He is uncompromising and demanding. He is not difficult in the same way as James Joyce – for example he doesn't make up new words as Joyce does. *A la recherche* is a novel in the mode of explanation and not of intellectualization. It is a reader's novel, not a writer's novel.

POINTS TO NOTE

* *Combray* is a wonderful piece of writing about childhood, whether you decide to go on and read the whole novel or not.

* *Un Amour de Swann* is one of the best analyses of jealous love ever written.

* The final section of the novel, *Le temps retrouvé*, contains Proust's theories on literature. These crucial sections of the work were all composed *at the same time*, around 1909–11.

* The other parts of *A la recherche* fill out Proust's overall conception. The novel is a kind of quest. The narrator of the book makes a series

of discoveries, which eventually enable him to start writing his own novel. *Le Côté de Guermantes* is about breaking into high society. *Sodome et Gomorrhe* is largely about the discovery of homosexuality. *La Prisonnière* and *Albertine disparue* are about loving and mourning – they work as a pair, and focus on just one other person, Albertine. *Le temps retrouvé* gives an account of Paris in the First World War.

* The different parts of the novel are separate from each other, but vital continuities run between them. Although the novel is narrated by one voice, a huge cast of characters wanders through its pages, fighting, loving, and getting older, more perverse, and more eccentric. After the summary of *A la recherche* there is a 'road map' (p. 47) which shows in graphic form how the novel works. You may find it useful to look at this now. It demonstrates the connections and continuities in the novel.

* Another continuity is provided by the sense that moral and psychological laws are being continuously recycled within the novel. Repetition is a key feature of this book. Proust would have been a brilliant writer for soap opera – with the difference that he wanted to show the *effects* of time passing, whereas soap opera seems to recycle a continuous present.

PROUST'S SENTENCES

Proust writes using unusually long sentences. He anchors what he wants to say to the main nouns in his sentences, and is then free to pursue his thoughts. Sometimes a single sentence runs to two pages. Yet Proust is not pretentious or wilfully digressive. There is a good reason for his long, open sentences. He seeks at all times to show *thought in action*. Reading and writing are *active* not *passive* processes for Proust. His writing depends on trains of associative thought, which build into very vivid impressions.

He is also, however, a sharp satirist and unnervingly accurate in his transactions with other people's weaknesses. The source of this satire is his ability to hoover up little splinters of detail about human behaviour, usually the giveaway signs that we think we are special and superior to others.

Proust hoovered up details about human nature.

If you try to pick out these minute details, rather than looking for plot progression, you will probably find that you are reading more slowly, but with more satisfaction. Don't be put off if you find that you forget half of what you read. Like pixels that build up an image which is only appreciable at a distance, each of Proust's sentences is individually significant, but also part of a bigger overall design. If you can bear to live with the intensity of Proust's focus, its contours will gradually stabilize.

Proust had to publish the first part of *A la recherche* himself, because he could find no one willing to take it. The reader at Ollendorff, a Parisian publisher, wrote, in early 1913, what was to become one of the most famous rejection letters of all time:

> My dear friend, I may be dead from the neck up, but rack my brains as I may, I fail to understand why a man needs thirty pages to describe how he tosses and turns in his bed before falling asleep.

Proust could see for himself that the book he had produced looked uncommercial. He knew it was a completely new way of presenting a novel, and was convinced it was good, but understood that it *looked* like a series of digressions, and that from a narrative point of view, the ideas in it didn't coalesce until much later than the first volume. Reading Proust is an act of faith, but there is a pay-off. Proust reminds us that we can never take anything for granted, but he also shows us how to cope with the chaotic pain that this inflicts on us.

FORM, CONTENT, AND STRUCTURE: AN OPENING FAN

Proust abandoned a critical essay, *Contre Sainte-Beuve* in around 1909, and decided that the novel, rather than the essay, was his preferred choice of form. This had an immediate impact upon the way he structured his writing. There is a difference between form and structure. We can say that a piece of literary writing will have a particular *form* – it'll be a play, or a novel, or a poem. But the *structure* of that form will vary. A play might have five acts, or consist of a monologue. Something that takes the form of a poem might have a three-line or a 3000-line structure. A novel may have 16 chapters, or no chapter breaks at all. Although structure doesn't only refer to the way something is broken into parts, it is a useful shorthand to differentiate *structure* from *form*.

Proust did not write in nice neat chapters

Proust wrote his novel in separable but interconnected *parts*, rather than chapters. Not all of these parts were planned out fully when he began his novel. So the structure of *A la recherche* doesn't really become clear with a glance at the contents page. Once you know that the beginning and the end were written at the same time, and that the novel expanded internally, you can think of the structure in the shape of an opening fan.

PROUST'S TECHNICAL ACHIEVEMENT

Proust made a major technical contribution to the novel form. He wrote his novel in the first person and in the past tense. This shifts our expectation of what novels do from 'telling' to 'showing'. Instead of *telling* a story ('he did this, then he went on to do that'), Proust *shows* his characters in action. You never have the sense, when you are reading Proust's novel, that the outcome of the story is already known, which is a remarkable feat for a book written in the past tense. You are always *in medias res*, in the thick of the situation, close up to the characters and their situations. Of course this caused Proust major technical problems. We can give this a name: his problem was that of *immediacy versus detachment.*

PROUST'S METAPHYSICAL PROBLEM

Proust was setting up a first-person narrator to look back over his past, while *simultaneously* living in the present, This means that Proust was tackling, head on, the tricky **metaphysical** problem that every one of us faces.

Getting to grips with time preoccupies us all. We cannot live in the past, yet we are inhabited by it, and cannot truly separate ourselves from it. We cannot live in the immediate present, since the present does not exist. The present is simply a continuous loss of the future to the past. It is not possible to 'seize the day'. The

KEYWORDS

Metaphysics literally means 'the works of the philosopher Aristotle written after his work on physics'. It is another word for ontology.

Ontology means the study of being, the attempt to analyse what it means to exist at all, and how we can grasp this meaning.

illusion that we can is the necessary paradox of being alive. Reflection reveals this impossibility to us, which is one of the reasons why reflection is painful. Even when we are in the act of realizing we cannot live in the present, it betrays us yet again by becoming the past. By the same token, we cannot live in the past, though we partially remember it, though we are constructed by it, and though it orders our priorities, perceptions, responses and desires, against our wills.

The fact that we *know* that we cannot go back, and cannot stand still, is at the base of much of our unhappiness, since it implies a further problem: we are all liars. It is not possible to be absolutely authentic or sincere, because there is no point in time or space from which to assert that here, now, I am telling the truth, I am myself, and I am completely honest. We are only provisional creatures, and the only truths we have available are unstable constructions. Having stated this as a technical and a metaphysical problem for Proust's overall project, it is easier to understand that, although Proust's novel is long, it is also supercharged with the intensity of taking on such a vital issue as its very substance. And what makes Proust brilliant lies in the fact that he *dramatizes* what might otherwise quickly become a suffocating or numbingly painful insight.

PROUST'S SOLUTION: UNDERSTANDING SELF–JUSTIFICATION

Proust's willingness to be captivated by other people and mesh them into his writing, his love of gossip, and his acute sense of how comedy flips over into tragedy or terror in human encounters, enable him to stop the novel being turgidly self-reflexive.

Proust's narrator is perpetually unravelling why it is that we cannot ever completely justify ourselves. For a long time, the narrator believes that unless he can somehow do this – and it is not clear to him how he would go about it, or to whom he needs to justify himself - he won't be able to begin his novel. Along the way, he gathers a huge amount of evidence about how other people get round this problem. In the end it is only when he stops justifying himself that writing can begin.

✱ ✱ ✱ ✱ *SUMMARY* ✱ ✱ ✱ ✱

- Proust's most important work is *A la recherche du temps perdu.*

- *A la recherche* is:
  - fiction not autobiography.
  - is a single continuous novel, around 3,000 pages long.
  - is written in the first person, and in the past tense.
  - is an investigation of subjective experience.

- Proust's style relies on long sentences, rich vocabulary, minute details and extended metaphors.

- *Combray* is an exploration of childhood.

- *Un Amour de Swann* is a brilliant analysis of jealousy.

- The final part, *Le temps retrouve*, was written at the same time as the opening, *Combray.*

Proust's biography: contexts and influences

3

SOME POLITICAL BACKGROUND

Proust lived through one of the most intensive periods in Europe's modern history: the last few decades of the nineteenth century, and the first two of the twentieth, just as France's revolutionary century, which had exploded in 1789, gave way to a new order. He was born in the suburbs of Paris on 10 July 1871, after the Second Empire had collapsed into the Third Republic.

PROUST'S EARLY LIFE

Marcel was a somewhat sickly child, and suffered asthma from the age of nine. Son of a brilliantly successful (and rather unimaginative) doctor father, Adrien Proust, and a gentle, well-read, protective mother, Jeanne Weil, Proust was also a religious hybrid: his mother was Jewish, his father Catholic. His Parisian childhood was uneventful. His brother Robert was two years younger than him. The family lived in an up-and-coming part of *rive droite* Paris, north of the River Seine, at 9, boulevard Malesherbes. They spent every Easter and part of the summer holidays in Illiers, a village just over 100 kilometres south-west of the capital.

KEY FACT

The Second Empire and the Third Republic
France lost Alsace and part of the Lorraine to the Germans in a humiliating peace settlement after losing to Bismarck at Sedan. From March to May of 1871, a Parisian revolutionary group who were christened the *Communards*, had staged an insurrection, brutally put down by a frightened and conservative new French régime.

SCHOOLDAYS AND BEYOND

Despite being absent through illness for much of the time, Marcel did pretty well at school, the prestigious Lycée Condorcet, where he spent rather a lot of his time ingratiating himself with the sons of aristocrats who were fellow pupils. He wrote for school magazines (the *Revue verte* and the *Revue lilas*), and was influenced by his philosophy teacher, Alphonse Darlu. As a teenager, he became infatuated with a 13-year-old girl, Marie de Bérnadaky, although homosexual preferences are also apparent from his letters. Proust was to love men as well as women – usually unhappily – throughout his life.

Happy days in the army.

While doing military service at Orléans, Proust slept in town, because his asthma prevented the other cadets sleeping. In 1890, he enrolled at two universities to study law as well as political theory. He received his *Licence en droit* (law degree) in 1893 and his *Licence ès lettres* (literature degree) in 1895. He was writing all the time, but *A la recherche du temps perdu* was still a long way off.

FIRST STEPS TO LITERARY SUCCESS

Proust led a double life while at university: student by day, social *arriviste* by night. Among various members of the European cultural élite encountered early on, he met Oscar Wilde briefly in 1891. Wilde announced that Proust's home was ugly. They didn't become friends.

Proust was starting to move in exclusive circles: he actively sought out the remnants of pre-Revolutionary French aristocracy. He helped to set up a literary magazine, *Le Banquet*, with some friends. He started to frequent salons. Jacques-Émile Blanche painted Proust's portrait. He developed huge crushes on elegant, intelligent women, but preferred to holiday at Trouville, on the Normandy coast, with young male friends.

In 1895, and under pressure from his father, he was offered a post at the Bibliothèque Mazarine. Due to begin as a librarian there in June, he pleaded ill health, on a basis which by 1900 had become permanent. He began instead to write fragments of *Jean Santeuil*. This was intended to be a novel, written in the third person, but heavily autobiographical.

THE DREYFUS AFFAIR

Proust's life took place in political terms against the backdrop of a chastened and cautious administration. One of the most important issues dominating France at the turn of the last century was the Dreyfus Affair, which lasted from 1894, when Proust was beginning to publish his early writing, until around 1906.

In January 1898, the writer Émile Zola published an open letter in *L'Aurore* to the French president, headed 'J'accuse', for which he was tried. The letter denounced the Government for not intervening on behalf of the falsely imprisoned Dreyfus. Proust attended Zola's trial, and wrote about it in *Jean Santeuil*. *L'Aurore* also published a petition signed by intellectuals, among them Proust, demanding that Dreyfus's case be re-opened.

KEY FACT

The Dreyfus Affair (1894–1906)
This minor military scandal erupted into a political fiasco that rocked the French nation, and triggered a major debate about anti-Semitism in France. A Jewish officer was framed and scape-goated in order to settle an investigation into army intelligence-gathering. But the set-up was itself exposed, and a massive campaign was mounted by the media and the intelligentsia in France, of both left and right wing persuasion, to exonerate Captain Dreyfus. It would not be an exaggeration to say that the Dreyfus Affair founds modern French history, and that its con-sequences are still apparent in debates surrounding French collaboration during World War Two.

Proust was what was known as a 'Dreyfusard', pro-Dreyfus, like his father. Having helped to organize the petition, however, he withdrew from political activism. He didn't withdraw his support for Dreyfus, but was intent on understanding how different parts of French society exploited the Affair for their own agendas.

FAMILY TROUBLES: CONSTRAINT AND FREEDOM

Proust's father died in November 1903 of a cerebral hæmorrhage. Proust was saddened but not incapacitated by his father's death. His beloved (though overpoweringly anxious) mother was now exclusively his. From 1904 to 1905, Proust was concentrating on an extended homage to the English art critic and socialist thinker, John Ruskin. Proust published one of his own most important theoretical essays, 'Sur la lecture' ('On Reading') early in 1905. This essay about reading was used in 1906 as the preface to Proust's translation of Ruskin's *Sesame and Lilies*. But tragedy was just about to interrupt this productive period.

PUNCTUATION IN A LIFE

His mother died of uremia in September 1905, and this loss was followed by a sustained period of grieving. Her death had other, more material, side effects. Proust was now the inheritor of a sizeable fortune, and no longer needed to earn a living (not that he'd done so before, never having turned up at the Bibliothèque Mazarine). Effectively, his way was paved to a full-time career as a writer. He set himself up in an uncle's apartment at 102, boulevard Haussmann, just a short distance from his childhood home. He was 34, grief-stricken, and completely unproductive. Even when he did manage to start writing again, what emerged was the rather macabre 'Sentiments filiaux d'un parricide' ('The Filial Feelings of a Parricide') published in *Le Figaro* in February 1907.

Proust loved his mother.

1908 – THE TURNING POINT

Proust suddenly began writing again in 1908, turning out a whole series of **pastiches** of famous nineteenth-century French writers and thinkers, all based on a single story about the forgery of diamonds, *l'Affaire Lemoine*.

He mimicked everyone from Balzac to Flaubert to Chateaubriand. The pastiches were mental gymnastics, limbering Proust up for what was about to happen, and freeing him of his literary forebears.

KEYWORD

Pastiche Literary imitation which points up the comedy in what is imitated.

WHICH WAY? LITERATURE OR CRITICISM?

By 1909, Proust was in the process of making a life-altering decision. He was working on a critical essay attacking Sainte-Beuve, the nineteenth-century French 'father' of literary criticism. This piece, left unfinished, was the most crucial gateway into *A la recherche*. The essay was conceived as a conversation with Proust's mother, but as Proust worked on it, characters and stories started to invade it, and eventually he abandoned it to start work on *A la recherche* in earnest.

His existence was from here on almost entirely given over to writing. The novel was written between 1908–9 and Proust's death in November 1922. Proust spent his whole adult life writing, the last half of it almost non-stop. Increasingly ill, and confined to bed, Proust wrote at night and became a near recluse in his cork-lined room. He exploited his illnesses to keep people away, or secure favours. A succession of young male secretaries and a devoted servant, Céleste Albaret, kept house for him, typing his wildly expanding manuscripts, while his friends indulged his hours and his eccentricities.

THE BEGINNING OF THE END
Between 1910 and 1911 Proust finished *A la recherche du temps perdu*. That is to say, he managed to nail into place the two planks that would ensure that all the rest of his writing was securely attached to a beginning and an end. The opening section of childhood scenes in an idyllic village was written *at the same time* as the last magnificent scene of the novel. The beginning looks back at childhood, and the ending looks forward to writing a novel based on the past. This is the structure of *A la recherche*, and everything else within it is supported by this simple two-pronged idea.

THE END OF THE BEGINNING
Proust established his reputation with the publication of *Du côté de chez Swann*, in late 1913. Two events obscured this publication, however, one with private, the other with public significance. In December 1913, Alfred Agostinelli, Proust's great obsession, who had been his chauffeur, and then one of his line of secretaries, ran away from his employer to Antibes, to become a pilot. He enrolled in the flying school under the pseudonym 'Marcel Swann'. By May 1914, he

was dead, drowned in a flying accident. Proust was distraught. In August 1914, the First World War started. Proust was not able to publish *A la recherche* continuously because Paris publishing houses shut down during the war.

Think of *A la recherche* in the shape of an opening fan.

By 1919 the novel had had a chance to expand internally by thousands of pages. While its essential structure never changed, it ballooned out, with a long section echoing Proust's mourning for the death of Agostinelli. An originally theoretical statement about the way we lose or waste time had been turned, by personal and political accident, into a graphic exploration of the time needed to recover from loss.

Proust died in November 1922 of pneumonia. By the time of his death, he had won the prestigious literary prize, the *prix Goncourt*, for the second part of his novel, *A l'ombre des jeunes filles en fleurs*, and had been elected a *chevalier de la Légion d'honneur*. His public recognition was late in coming but absolute. After his death, his brother Robert undertook the massive task of publishing the remaining parts of his novel. He is buried in the Père Lachaise cemetery in Paris.

✳ ✳ ✳ ✳ *SUMMARY* ✳ ✳ ✳ ✳

- Proust was born into the *haute bourgeoisie*, the upper middle class, at a time of political upheaval which founded France's Third Republic.

- His early life was marked by ill health, success at school and university, and social aspirations.

- He inherited enough money to write full time at the age of 34.

- There was no sign of *A la recherche du temps perdu* until he was around 38 years old.

Proust's major works

4

EARLY WRITING: FRAGMENTS AND FOUNDATIONS

Before looking at *A la recherche* in more detail, we should think about some of the early themes and subjects preoccupying Proust. This will show how sustained Proust's thinking was, and how major parts of his thought took shape before *A la recherche* was conceived and executed.

Jean Santeuil (1895–99)

This was Proust's first attempt at a novel. He worked on it for four years. It was left unfinished, and was written in the third person. It is a semi-autobiographical fiction, and demonstrates how Proust proceeded by working up fragments which eventually interconnected, rather than planning a structure in advance and then filling it in. There are obvious crossovers with *A la recherche du temps perdu*: the protagonist is a young man making his way in Third Republic French aristocratic society. There are accounts of the Dreyfus Affair and Émile Zola's trial. There are tales of frustrated love affairs. On the whole, however, *Jean Santeuil* was left behind once *A la recherche* was underway, and is very much the work of an immature writer. The style is influenced by late-nineteenth-century **decadence**. *Jean Santeuil* was finally published long after Proust's death.

Les Plaisirs et les Jours (*Pleasures and Days*), 1896

More *fin de siècle* decadence (Proust was getting it out of his system). This was a collection of short stories that focus on sexual perversity among members of the aristocratic

KEYWORD

Decadence a literary attitude evident in nineteenth-century French Symbolist poetry and literature. Symbolist poetry emphasized sensationalism, the grotesque, the exotic, melodrama and ego-centricity. The artist saw himself as an 'outsider'. Decadent writers and poets felt that they were suffering from a kind of illness, *ennui*. This literally means both 'boredom' and 'embarrassment'. It was used by the decadents to refer to *fin de siècle* (literally 'end of the century') distaste for contemporary bourgeois life, which was materialistic and a bit smug.

classes. They were pretentious – their publication earned Proust a lot of sniping and his reputation for being a snob and a social climber.

Sur la lecture (On Reading), 1905

This was the important preface to a translation of Ruskin's *Sesame and Lilies*. The translation was undertaken by Proust with the help of a friend, Marie Nordlinger. Reading is, for Proust, a two-way activity, catalyzing our own thoughts, rather than a passive acceptance of somebody else's thought:

> We feel very clearly that our own wisdom begins where that of the author leaves off, and would like him to provide us with answers, when all he can do is provide us with desires.

Pastiches (1908)

This is a series of imitations, based on a scandal surrounding a diamond forgery, called *l'affaire Lemoine*. By parodying the styles of famous French novelists like Balzac and Flaubert, Proust was purging himself of their influence over his own style. They were published posthumously as part of *Pastiches et mélanges*.

Contre Sainte-Beuve (1908–9)

This work is half essay, half notes for a novel. The artist's output, implied the nineteenth-century critic Sainte-Beuve, could be fully understood by knowing lots of anecdotes about his life, reading his letters, and knowing what he had for breakfast. Proust argued that the artist's lived life is irrelevant to understanding the ideas in his books. Biography might be interesting, but will not supply us with understanding. This is a crucial idea in twentieth-century literary theory.

Proust wrote neither **biography** nor **auto-biography**. He wrote *fiction*. The secret of tackling the complexity of reading *A la recherche du temps perdu* is to remember that it is NOT a straightforward, chronological account of Proust's life.

KEYWORDS

Biography versus auto-biography 'Biography' literally means 'life writing', while 'auto-bio-graphy' means 'self life writing', or a life written by the person who lived it.

Introduction to *A La Recherche Du temps Perdu*

5

This chapter will show you some of the main points to think about when tackling *A la recherche* by looking at the first two parts of the work: *Combray* and *Un Amour de Swann*. Later chapters will outline the main plot and major themes.

A la recherche can be summarized quite quickly, in fact, by saying that it is the story of a would-be writer, which ends at the moment that he begins his novel – we never actually find out what the narrator is working on. Yet it is not an account of writer's block, as much as a revelation of *metamorphosis*.

THE TITLE

In thinking about how to get to grips with *A la recherche*, there is no better place to start than Proust's title. *A la recherche du temps perdu* is actually difficult to translate into English. It looks as though it means 'In Search of Lost Time'. But we hit the problem with 'perdu', which does mean 'lost', but also means 'wasted'. The first English translation skirted around this ambiguity, by using a quotation from Shakespeare: *Remembrance of Things Past*. Proust was understandably unhappy about this mistake. His novel is not really about things in the past. It is a massive investigation of the techniques we might try to use to retrieve subjective experience.

The last thing Proust wanted was to ramble on nostalgically about his own past – though he was not above laughing at the rest of us for doing so on a semi-permanent basis. He wanted to understand how memory works, not write his memoirs.

THE OPENING LINE OF *A LA RECHERCHE*

The next important dimension of Proust's work appears in the very first line of *Combray*. The novel starts in the **first-person voice**.

Here is the first sentence, in French and in English.

> *Longtemps, je me suis couché de bonne heure.*
> For a long time, I went to bed early.

This is a very odd opening. There is nothing to situate us. We know nothing about the narrator – not even whether a man or a woman is speaking. We do not know whether this is fiction or autobiography. We do not know whether 'Combray' is a person or a place. We have no idea WHEN or WHY the narrator went to bed early – as a child, or later in life, whether because of illness or laziness, how long this period of going to bed early lasted. The novel opens on an enigma – how is Proust going to hold our attention for 3,000 pages?

KEYWORDS

First-person voice writing directly about subjective, or personal, experience using the 'I' voice. Confessional narratives and autobiographies are in the first person.

Selfhood the way we understand ourselves as having an individual character and existence, separate from anybody else's.

IDENTITY CONFUSION

The trick is to think about this novel another way. Proust is asking us to think about how we understand *identity*. He goes on to point out that when we are in that border zone between waking and sleeping, we sometimes identify ourselves with the things we have just been thinking about. Here's how he phrases it: 'I would have the impression that I myself was what the book was talking about'. This confusion of identities is Proust's theory of **selfhood** in action.

It is absolutely crucial to understanding how *A la recherche* works to grasp what is going on here. The way Proust achieves the effect of identity confusion is not by having his narrator say 'sometimes we don't know who we are'. Proust has taken out conventional

framing devices. The explanatory sentences, which might reassure us that the narrator is not wasting our time, are deliberately missing. He doesn't say, for example 'I would have the impression that I myself was what the book was talking about – but dismiss it as irrational, and go off to do the washing up'.

> **KEYWORD**
>
> Framing devices items such as nouns, facts, dates, times and orders of events, in sentences or whole stories, which structure them, and make them 'safe', i.e. credible.

By omitting a rational disclaimer in this way, Proust instantly ensures that the narrator's credibility in our eyes can only be guaranteed by the *authenticity* of what he has to say. In other words, he will only be trustworthy... if we trust him. And we will only trust him if we agree that sometimes identity can feel unstable. Proust is setting up an intensely intimate environment for his narrator, and for us. He is actively demanding our trust. *A la recherche* would be impossible to read unless we acknowledged a degree of personal vulnerability.

A THEORY OF READING AND WRITING

The book begins with a description of what it is like to read. Because we are also readers, we are immediately sucked into an intimate collaboration with the narrator. *A la recherche* opens, in other words, with a **theory**, not a *story*.

> **KEYWORD**
>
> Theory literally, a way of seeing something, a model, design, or perspective attempting to describe or control reality.

Proust makes sure that we cannot quite decide whether the narrator is a bit odd – or whether he is making an empirical study of the effects of sleep, using himself as a laboratory experiment, on behalf of all of us. We are drawn in despite our better judgement.

There is another way to think about this opening, which will become more important as *Combray* unfolds. We are being shown, from the very first line, the processes by which someone comes to write about childhood. In other words, the opening is as much about the technical impossibility of remembering past events accurately or completely as it is about the events being described. With the difficulties of retrospection come the difficulties of finding a style and a structure that will map out what the narrator wants to say about looking back over past events.

Should the style reflect a child's perspective or the writing adult's point of view? What kind of words should you use to convey the intensity of a childhood emotion, when you are looking back at it from the comparative safety of adulthood?

Proust sets up a blank canvas for himself, and uses a description of the way sleep can destabilize us to do so. The dreaming state, for Proust, is an immensely privileged state of vulnerability. We co-exist, when we are asleep and dreaming, with our own pasts, to such an extent that we do not know where or who we are when we wake up.

TECHNIQUES DEVELOPED IN *COMBRAY*

The opening of *A la recherche* can be seen as a kind of initiation ceremony. Proust's narrator takes us through a succession of rooms remembered from his past, as an **analogy** for the experience of waking up.

> **KEYWORD**
>
> **Analogy** a likeness found between different things. A metaphor is an analogy in which the qualities of one thing are swapped for the qualities of another.

But instead of getting up, the narrator carries on lying in bed trawling through memories. Quite unexpectedly he takes us to Combray, apparently a place where he had been as a child.

The magic lantern

The first thing the narrator tells us about himself as a little boy in Combray is that his family used to try to cheer him up when he was unhappy with a 'lanterne magique', a magic lantern that projected images from a popular story onto the wall. The popular story, however, is somewhat sinister. It is about a medieval lady, Geneviève de Brabant, who has to defend her honour against a predatory suitor, Golo, while

The magic lantern at Combray.

her husband is absent. The magic lantern frightens the child for two reasons: one because the projected images seem supernatural, but secondly because the child identifies himself with the would-be rapist Golo. He runs to his mother for comfort, but also for absolution – yet has committed no visible crime.

Within the first ten pages of the novel, reading, dreaming, waking, remembering, and feeling guilty are virtually the only actions we have come across. They all share the characteristic of being mental activities which demand concentration, but which we cannot completely control.

Proust's economy of style

The dinner bell that ends the ordeal of the magic lantern turns out to be the fragile link to a different memory, or set of memories (we cannot tell). These are the after-dinner habits of the family at Combray. Tiny connections, like the sound of the dinner bell, from one moment of the narrative to another, are common in *A la recherche*. They are active demonstrations of how the memory functions through association. They are also cannily economical ways to structure a story, by moving from one intense point of focus to another.

Proust's style is surprisingly economical in other ways as well. Not a single word in his narrative is redundant. Here is the way the narrator's family is described. The child's father consults the barometer; the mother gazes fondly at him, but not too analytically; the grandmother walks resolutely out in the garden even when it is pouring with rain – unless her sisters tell her that her husband is drinking forbidden brandy, to tease her, when she rushes indoors, but always fails to stop him. Within the space of a page, we understand that the father is self-important, the mother self-effacing, and the grandmother honest and naïve, though Proust has not told us this explicitly. We have gleaned this information from a series of microscopic images and details, utterly banal in themselves, but in Proust's hands, instruments which reveal character. He wanted this to be seen as *kaleidoscopic*.

The imperfect tense

His economical methods don't stop with characterization. They are exhibited in the tense in which he is writing. He often writes in the **imperfect tense**.

The use of the imperfect tense is a compressed way to convey several years in a paragraph, and it leaves Proust free to zoom in and out of his narrative, homing in on particular incidents, without needing to supply a firm context.

> **KEYWORD**
>
> Imperfect tense used for habitual actions in the past, going on for an indefinite length of time, or at an unspecified time, e.g. 'We used to travel a lot'. Another form of past tense is the past historic, e.g. 'We went travelling last year'. It is used for actions completed at a specific time in the past.

The opening pages of the novel are uncompromising: we are being taken into one person's world, and there are few concessions to 'normal' plot development. It is hard to see where this book will take us, and we find ourselves completely in the hands of this first-person narrator, drifting along in the imperfect tense, without markers or frameworks, halfway between dreaming and remembering.

The goodnight kiss

Yet there is also something intense about the narration. The next major incident is famously called the *drame du coucher*, literally the 'bedtime drama', or more often the 'Goodnight Kiss' episode. The little boy's one consolation about being sent to bed is that his mother usually gives him a goodnight kiss. But when the family has 'visitors' (there is actually only ever one, Swann, and we will come back to him) she does not come to his bedroom.

No goodnight kiss (with apologies to E.H. Shepherd).

In the narration of this incident we move suddenly from the general to the particular – this is not the dreamy evocation of years of childhood, but the agonizing recall of one particular evening. Because it is still written in the imperfect tense, however, we are unlikely to realize how urgent and specific this anecdote is until it has nearly played itself out.

On this particular occasion, the little boy has been anticipating the goodnight kiss, which he knows will be briefer than usual, because of

Swann's presence. Abruptly his father orders him to go to bed, without the kiss, but he desperately lies in wait for his mother, and launches himself at her when she comes upstairs. She is angry, and tries to make him hide before he is seen by his father – but it is too late. His father is known to be strict but arbitrary. And now this unpredictability makes itself felt, but in a wholly new way: his father nonchalantly gives in to the child's anxieties, and allows his wife to spend the night with her son. The child's nervousness is being interpreted, for the first time, not as a fault to be punished but as an involuntary failing for which he is not responsible. Instead of happiness, however, the child feels that a concession has been made which has damaged the ideal image of himself his mother would like to help him attain. The victory is against her.

Right at the beginning of the novel, then, we are being shown a child's world in which passionate, uncontrollable needs and anxieties are given the highest priority. A ritual goodnight kiss is one thing, but this version of it is quite clearly being set up as a founding moment in the child's life. Using his emotions to manipulate his parents, he succeeded in obtaining what he wanted, but simultaneously altered their perception of his character forever. Memories are not rose-tinted; they are evidence of life-altering modifications of our whole identity. We are, or Proust's narrator wants us to accept that we are, in the grip of such founding memories.

Voluntary memory

If memories were only the recall of events, which, in traumatizing us, have changed the course of our lives, *A la recherche* would have been a great deal shorter. There is something fishy about the goodnight kiss episode. Surely traumatic memories are the ones that are obliterated by our protective conscious minds, though they return to us in nightmares, or may mark our actions? Proust's narrator seems to have kicked off with the deepest, most psychologically scarring memory. He tells us that all he has left of his childhood is a fixed image of 'two storeys linked by a narrow staircase', where it is always seven o'clock at night. This he calls 'voluntary memory', his conscious recall. The capital importance of the goodnight kiss is, however, about to be swept away by another kind of memory altogether. This is the message of the famous *madeleine* scene.

The *madeleine* dipped in lime-blossom tea

The narrator is minding his own business one day, when his mother, seeing how cold he is, offers to make him some tea. At first he refuses, but then for no good reason, accepts. His mother sends for *madeleine* cakes, which are plump little sponge cakes baked in a mould the shape of a *coquille Saint-Jacques* shell. He happens to dip a piece in a teaspoonful of tea, and absentmindedly eats the resulting mix. Instantly, he is overwhelmed by a sense of pleasure, almost as if he were in love. The sense of release, however, has not come from the outside in, but is moving from the inside out, as if the *madeleine*-tea mix has simply been the catalyst to an essential part of himself which is now revealed.

But what has been revealed? The narrator finds that when he relaxes rather than concentrates, a memory of his aunt Léonie offering him *madeleine* soaked in lime-blossom tea, when he was a child in Combray, pops into his head. It is the sensation of taste that has preserved this image, but it has taken a chance repetition of the sensation to reproduce the memory intact. With this image, the narrator finds, unfurling like Japanese paper flowers that open when they are dipped in water, or like the dried lime-blossom flowers that release their preserved flavour in boiling water, the whole of Combray, village, people, parks, houses, all of it, seeping into his memory as though they were the fragrance of his steaming cup of tea. This is involuntary memory, and it is fundamental to Proust's whole project that we should understand that *involuntary* memory is more important than *voluntary* memory.

This is complex stuff. Are we to understand that all the narrator could remember of his childhood was one traumatic night, until he ate a cake? Surely the unpleasant memory of his childhood neurosis is more

And just as in that game the Japanese like so much,
> dipping tiny twists of paper in a porcelain bowl
filled with water ...

> houses, substantial and recognizable people,
and now even all the flowers in our garden
> and the ones in Monsieur Swann's park,
and the waterlilies in the Vivonne,
> and the good burghers of the village
> and their little homes
> and the church
> and the whole of Combray
and its surroundings,
> all of that material solidity
> came out, town and gardens,
> of my

> cup
of
> tea.

The narrator's memories unfurl from his cup of tea.

important for self-understanding than remembering his aunt feeding him soggy sponge? The point Proust is trying to make is to do with *abundance* and *spontaneity*. His conscious recall gave him only the nasty little image of being humiliated by his father. His unconscious recall, however, could restore all of his life in the village, as it had been, good, bad, and indifferent – without the distortion of later analysis. Memory of psychological damage is not the only kind of memory but it may discolour our happier experiences. The reduction of our pasts to a single unhappy image is a truly terrible loss, and Proust's goal is to give us methods for recovering the full range of our experience. He is reminding us that we work on half power too much of the time.

THE DEVELOPMENT OF THE *COMBRAY* SECTION

Combray sets up all the important stories, theories, and characters that *A la recherche* will pursue. Above all, it gives us a chance to get used to Proust's long sinuous sentences, with their multiple clauses, and to realize that Proust's style is not separable from his subject-matter. We will now look at what is covered in *Combray*.

After the *madeleine* moment, *Combray*, released from the narrator's cup of tea, consists of a languorous, drifting evocation of village life and characters. We find descriptions of the narrator's hypochondriac aunt Léonie, manipulating the narrator's family from her bed. We are introduced to the local church, the parishioners, family dinnertime habits, accounts of the servants, reading as a boy in the garden (identifying himself with everything he reads), and, most importantly, going for country walks.

It is an idyllic-sounding childhood, and it is not surprising that many people conclude that *A la recherche* is about nostalgia, from reading this part of the novel.

Indeed, Proust is perfectly explicit about this: he insists that true paradises are the ones we have already irretrievably lost. This maxim shouldn't, however, be interpreted to mean that *A la recherche* is a long regretful whinge. It is a much more powerful summation of the difficulties of managing time. Proust suggests that we simply cannot comprehend experiences until they are over. Put another way, while we might know that we are happy or unhappy, we cannot explain exactly why – without ending that state.

Which way? Sex or society?

The country walks generally take two directions. There is Swann's way, the route that takes the narrator's family past Swann's estate, Tansonville, and there is the Guermantes way, the path that leads along the banks of the Vivonne River. Each route gives rise to radically different kinds of association and experience for the narrator, both as a child, and in his remembrance of them.

Swann's way is associated with Proust's exploration of bourgeois society. It is also associated with private sexuality, including homosexuality, and questions of morality. It is when he is walking along Swann's way that the narrator sees Gilberte, the daughter of Swann and Odette, for the first time. She is later to become his first love. Proust's theory of sexual desire is that we love on the basis of a prototype, which is never fully abandoned. First loves are the way we love. Gilberte is a prototype of Albertine, the narrator's most important lover.

The Guermantes way is associated with public, aristocratic society, and dreams of becoming a writer – experiments in converting impressions to linguistic expressions. The Guermantes are an aristocratic family with land near Combray. The narrator sees members of the family in the village church, and fantasizes about winning the love of the haughty duchesse de Guermantes. The next major section of *A la recherche* will describe the narrator's attempts to break into high society in Paris, and his eventual success, when he is invited to the prince and princesse de Guermantes's parties.

After the narrator's family has been out walking along the Guermantes way one day, the narrator attempts his first piece of serious writing. It is about the church steeples of a village called Martinville. They seem to exchange places and dance as they are viewed from the moving coach of Dr Percepied, who is giving the narrator's family a lift home.

The two ways united

The two walks and their associations seem irreconcilable. This is not, however, always to be the case, something which has vital repercussions on our understanding of *A la recherche* as a single complex novel, rather than a series of discrete stories linked by one man's strenuous will and publicity campaign. Towards the end of the novel, the narrator visits his one-time love, Gilberte Swann, who has since married Saint-Loup, a close friend of the narrator's, and is living at Tansonville, Swann's estate. She tells the narrator that the two ways are linked geographically. The narrator could have walked in a big circle. His sense that the two ways went in diametrically opposite directions was based on his own limited subjective perspective – an assumption based on turning left or right outside his own front door.

Two different directions may be *divergent* rather than *opposite*, and may be reunited further down the line. This union of two ways is one of the grand metaphors of the novel, and is reflected in countless other parts of it. Voluntary and involuntary memory are not quite separable. Heterosexuality is different from homosexuality – but only just. Language and experience are inextricably linked. Gilberte is like Albertine is like the narrator's mother – but not quite. Gilberte's marriage to the aristocrat Saint-Loup itself represents the union of two class systems. The novel as a whole documents the way the French middle class seeped into the aristocratic upper class throughout the Third Republic, especially as a result of the First World War, but also because of intermarriages.

SWANN IN LOVE

If we move on to the second part of *Du côté de chez Swann*, which is called *Un Amour de Swann*, or *Swann in Love*, we find that it is, paradoxically, written in the third person – the narrator suddenly intervenes upon the tale of his own childhood to tell us Swann's story. Previously we have only known Swann as the visitor to the narrator's family at Combray, and the source of the narrator's misery: whenever he comes for dinner, the child is deprived of his goodnight kiss. Now we see Swann in a completely different light. Proust's method of characterization is to show how people co-exist as different versions of themselves. Here is an account of how the second part of the first section of *A la recherche* works.

Un Amour de Swann is a story about a jealous love affair. It lays the groundwork for Proust's account of love and snobbery throughout *A la recherche*. The two themes are related through the idea of *exclusion*. For Proust, love works through lack. Whatever you are excluded from, you desire. Social climbing works in the same way.

Swann's story, although it is not explicitly dated, seems to take place at the end of the nineteenth century, before the birth of the narrator (the source of the narrator's information about Swann remains something of a mystery). He is a well-to-do Parisian gentleman, whose main activities are womanizing and socializing. He occupies his spare time with writing an account of the seventeenth-century Dutch painter Vermeer. Vermeer, famous to us for his mysterious, **allegorical** interiors, was virtually unknown as late as the 1880s. So Swann's interest in Vermeer shows him to have extensive knowledge about art.

KEYWORD

Allegory literally 'speaking otherwise'. A story with a double meaning, which operates at two or more levels, for example *Pilgrim's Progress* by John Bunyan.

Earlier in the novel, we see Swann comparing a servant in the narrator's household with one of Giotto's early fourteenth-century Virtues and Vices from the Arena Chapel in Padua, Italy. Giotto was famous for re-introducing natural models for allegorical or moral effect. His paintings look as though they are based on personal experience, and convey an unusual psychological intensity. Both Vermeer and Giotto were important artists for Proust, who also emphasized quiet small details, and psychological insight.

The inverted snob: Mme Verdurin

Swann meets Odette through a couple called The Verdurins, who are Proust's comic masterpieces of idiotic pretension. Swann is appalled by their vulgarity, but puts up with it in order to enjoy the favours of their little friend Odette. Madame Verdurin, an overbearing social climber, cultivates a salon of mediocre talents. She is forever compensating for the inadequacies of her entourage with elaborately staged, jaw-dislocating laughter, and fabricated neuralgia. She calls her faithful adherents her *petit clan* and all the salons by which she is excluded are designated *les ennuyeux*.

Her excessive reactions are an index of her excessive desire for social recognition. She is one of the most famous examples in European literature of the inverted snob.

Desire is based on lack

Swann is easily able to keep his own exclusive connections separate from the Verdurins' envious, acquisitive gaze while he is detached from the spectacle of snobbery. Where he comes unstuck is through his taste for artistic analogies. He starts telling himself that Odette looks like a Botticelli painting (of Zipporah, Jethro's daughter), because it flatters his sensibilities to do so. When he hears a Sonata by Vinteuil (a fictional composer whose work comes to play a crucial part in the narrator's evaluation of the worth of art in general) Swann elects one moment in it to be the 'national anthem' of his love affair. He makes emblems for what he feels because he does not feel anything much. It is not until he is suddenly deprived of Odette one evening, when she fails to appear at the Verdurins, that he realizes that he does not fully control her movements, and that his own insecurities come into play.

Proust is making the point that we want precisely what we do not have. Desire is based on lack, and driven by need. That need, for Proust, is the need to *know*. Swann displays the quintessential Proustian mixture of jealousy and envy. *Jealousy* is what we feel when we think someone is trying to take away what we have. *Envy* is defined as wanting what someone else has.

Jealousy and envy

Swann gradually slides into a state of jealousy about Odette's other suitors and also a paralysing envy of her past life, a life which he will never fully understand. Proust doesn't just state this, he enacts it, imitating Swann's increasing obsession by recording in ever greater detail the minutiae of Swann's activities – the letters, the spying, the interrogations, the indifference to all that does not concern Odette. Swann gradually realizes that despite his monitoring (or perhaps because of it), Odette continues to have other lovers, notably Forcheville. He tries to cure himself of his compulsive love, but it is too far gone. One day he hears the little phrase from the Vinteuil Sonata, which he had designated the national anthem of his love affair. The repetition of this allows him to recognize that the affair is over.

Yet this is not the end of either the relationship or the story. We are subjected to the intermittent jealousy and flat indifference Swann experiences, as his perspective reverts to its original state. Proust does not end stories at their most dramatic climax. One sense in which he is a new kind of *realist* writer is that he narrates the banality of *anticlimax*. He embeds stories within contexts. In the next part of *A la recherche*, we are astonished to find that Swann has married Odette, and has a daughter, Gilberte.

Swann's use of art

Swann's taste for comparison and collection, his sophisticated ability to draw parallels between famous works of art and living people, turns out to be his undoing. He moves too easily between art and people, and he moves in the wrong direction. People make art, art does not make people. Swann is doomed never to realize that his method of gentrifying, or æstheticizing, the ordinary stuff of life is only a way of freezing it, rather than a way of understanding it. For all his discriminating prowess, he does not know how to discern what is valuable in either life or art.

Desire and the mind

Swann is a stereotypical late-nineteenth-century caricature, a type which appeared in a lot of Proust's early writing. But his purpose in *A la recherche du temps perdu* is far more complex than simple caricature. Proust zooms in on an account of Swann's affair with Odette. Swann's jealous obsession with a woman who, on the face of it, is not even to Swann's taste, demonstrates something else entirely. Swann is an experiment in how sexual desire colonizes and modifies intellectual analysis.

A greater purpose is building behind this account. Swann is being set up as a rival and a pre-figuration for the narrator himself, who, in *Sodome et Gomorrhe, La Prisonnière*, and *Albertine disparue*, has exactly the same kind of jealous affair with Albertine, and who is driven to even greater excesses. He virtually imprisons Albertine in his Paris apartment. Swann's purpose in the novel is to be trumped by the narrator, who suffers the same jealous blindness, but wins the insight of art.

✳ ✳ ✳ ✳SUMMARY✳ ✳ ✳ ✳

- Use of the first-person confessional form sets up complicity between narrator and reader.

- Proust writes surprisingly economically, using associative connections, tiny details, and the imperfect tense.

- Proust presents different kinds of memory: voluntary and involuntary.

- *Combray* details the narrator's childhood life.

- The two different walks of the narrator's childhood set up a binary quest which governs the whole novel: love and society versus art. When he discovers they are united, he realizes that nothing is stopping him from writing.

- *Un Amour de Swann* is written in the third person.

- Swann's jealous love affair is a prototype for the narrator's affair with Albertine.

- Swann's lesson to the narrator is that people make art, but art doesn't make people.

6 The 'Summarize Proust' Competition

Having established some of the ways in which Proust's style is inseparable from his subject matter, it is much easier to follow the complexities of the plot. This section briefly summarizes the way the book develops. The chapters that come after it will look at certain ideas and themes more closely.

This summary is designed to show that *A la recherche* is a single, continuous novel, broken into irregular chunks, not chapters. You can also look at the 'road map' on page 47 to help you see the structure.

After the section on Swann, we revert to the first-person narrative voice. The narrator dreams of visiting Balbec, a seaside resort. By now the narrator's family are living in Paris, and we see the little boy playing with Gilberte – who turns out to be the daughter of Swann and Odette. We realize they are now married. The young narrator falls in love with Gilberte.

IN *A L'OMBRE DES JEUNES FILLES EN FLEURS* (LITERALLY, *IN THE SHADE OF BLOSSOMING GIRLS*) ...

The narrator announces a change of direction for his 'characters'. This is an odd term, because they are the narrator's contemporaries – he undermines the convention by which we accept that he has not yet started writing. This is a good example of the ambiguous double voice that narrates *A la recherche*, simultaneously inside the fiction and writing it.

Norpois

We meet Norpois the diplomat for the first time. He comes to dinner with the narrator's family. The narrator has just seen an actress called La Berma perform in Racine's *Phèdre*, but cannot form an opinion of her performance. He asks Norpois for an opinion of La Berma and his own writing. Norpois is condescending, and the narrator, believing himself talentless, is put off completely, though his father has finally accepted that he can do nothing except be a writer.

Juvenile infatuation
The narrator is still in love with Gilberte, and there is a long section detailing the pleasures and anxieties of juvenile infatuation. It dovetails with an account of Odette's salon. Swann has become slightly coarsened by his marriage: he champions Odette's second-rate salon, into which the narrator is welcomed. Odette plays him Vinteuil's Sonata, which had held such significance for Swann. It is one of the ways in which Swann and the narrator are intimately connected. The narrator meets his favourite writer Bergotte at one of Odette's lunch parties. The disparity between his odd voice and bulbous nose, and his writing, disappoints the narrator.

The narrator goes to a brothel with his friend Bloch. He breaks up with Gilberte. There is a long period of renunciation, until he realizes suddenly that he has recovered and is indifferent to Gilberte.

First separation from mother
He goes to Balbec with his grandmother, and the servant Françoise. His childhood dreams of adventure merge with adolescent sexual fantasies – this trip marks his first separation from his mother. There are hilarious descriptions of hotel life. The clients and valets are a fully-formed social microcosm. The hotel takes on the marine characteristics of its environment: the restaurant is like an aquarium. At the coast, the grandmother meets an old friend, Madame de Villeparisis, who is related to the prestigious Guermantes family. The narrator is desperately hoping for both sexual and aristocratic encounters. He goes out driving with Madame de Villeparisis, visiting local Normandy churches. Finally he is introduced to Robert de Saint-Loup, Madame de Villeparisis's nephew. The narrator makes embarrassed comparisons between his new-found friend, and Bloch, the defiantly vulgar Jewish

upstart. At the same time, he is aware of a shadowy figure who will go on to dominate the later part of the novel: Baron Charlus. The narrator is caught between classes.

The blossoming girls and Elstir the painter

One day he spots a group of athletic young girls, like a flock of gulls, moving as one down the promenade. He catches the eye of a girl in a polo cap, just as Gilberte had caught his eye in Combray. It is Albertine. Unable to meet the girls, he is consoled by inebriated dinners at Rivebelle with Saint-Loup. There he meets the painter Elstir. At first he cannot understand Elstir's work. Then he realizes that Elstir's æsthetic is to paint things as they first appear to him: to paint his impressions. He sees a portrait of 'Miss Sacripant', a woman dressed as a man. It is Odette, one of many representations of her that are interpersed through the novel. She is always depicted as a male fantasy.

Finally he meets the group of young girls. Albertine singles him out. He spends more and more time with the group, as an honorary girl. He is in love with all of them, at once and in succession. Eventually he becomes more attracted to Albertine, but when she invites him to her hotel room, she refuses to kiss him. Gradually the mystery that surrounds the young girls resolves itself into a more stable understanding of their class and type. The summer also gives way to the sombre clarity of autumn.

BACK IN PARIS, WE BEGIN *LE CÔTÉ DE GUERMANTES* (ROUGHLY, *THE GUERMANTES WAY*) ...

The narrator's family has moved to a flat in the Guermantes's property. The narrator goes to see La Berma perform in *Phèdre* again, at the Opéra. He is hoping to spy the duchesse de Guermantes, rather than admire the acting. Detached from the performance, he understands that La Berma's creativity lies in her subjective interpretation of the role, as Elstir's did in his painting. The duchesse inadvertently smiles at the narrator. He is instantly besotted. He travels to the garrison town of Doncières where Saint-Loup is an army officer, to ask for an introduction to the duchesse. During the visit, he becomes fascinated by the long discussions of military strategy. A pretext is found for seeing the duchesse de Guermantes: to look at her collection of Elstir paintings. Saint-Loup's behaviour towards other men is inexplicably violent.

Grandmother's illness

The narrator returns to Paris, at a loose end. His grandmother is ill, he cannot write, he is not invited into salon life. Saint-Loup comes back on leave, and they visit his lover, Rachel. Saint-Loup is aggressive and jealous towards her. They watch her act, and Saint-Loup exhibits more unpredictable behaviour, slapping a journalist.

Finally, the narrator is invited to Madame de Villeparisis's salon. Bloch, Norpois and Legrandin, another social climber, are all there. The Guermantes appear. The Dreyfus Affair is at its height, and divides the salon. There is a long sequence of party chatter. The entry of Charlus reminds the narrator of a bizarre encounter with Morel (who is to play an important part in Charlus's life), an ambitious valet turned violinist. The narrator finds out that his uncle Adolphe had kept a collection of pornographic photographs, notably of Odette. Charlus is the duc de Guermantes's brother. Charlus offers to act as mentor to the narrator. He seems out of control, relishing an anti-Semitic tirade on the subject of Bloch.

Social and sexual conquests

The narrator's grandmother is seriously ill. While out with the narrator, she has a slight stroke. She is dying. After her death, the narrator starts to search out sexual favours in earnest. Albertine comes to visit. She has matured. The narrator is attracted, although he is not in love. They finally kiss. Triumphant, the narrator makes an excellent impression on the duchesse de Guermantes at a soirée, because he is no longer attracted to her. She instantly invites him to dinner. The narrator, sure of Albertine's affections, tries to seduce Madame de

Stermaria, but she flatly rejects him. The narrator howls with
frustration. Saint-Loup takes him out to dinner with other young
aristocrats. Their nonchalant grace and athleticism fascinates the
narrator, though he secretly thinks that friendship is a self-indulgent
distraction from the rigours of writing.

Dinner with the Guermantes

The narrator goes to dinner with the Guermantes. He is late because he
spends too long admiring their collection of Elstir paintings. He is
introduced to aristocrats he has dreamt of, and is suitably disappointed
by their fatuous ritualized manners. Nevertheless he spends a great deal
of time analysing their genealogies, kinship structures and witty
conversation. Their opinions on art are based on acquisition not
interpretation. At the end of the dinner, the narrator visits Charlus,
who condescendingly taunts him. The narrator furiously stamps on
the baron's top hat.

Later, the narrator receives an invitation to a party given by the prince
and princesse de Guermantes – he has reached the pinnacle of
aristocratic society. Unsure whether the invitation is real, he goes to ask
the duc and duchesse, but far from reassuring him, they become
defensive. He realizes that exposing vulnerability makes them mistrust
him, rather than building friendship. Swann arrives. The duc and
duchesse are in a hurry to leave for a party before a cousin of theirs
dies, so that they won't have to miss it. They impatiently brush aside
Swann's news that he is also dying, yet find the time for the duchesse to
change her shoes even after they have got into their carriage.

SODOME ET GOMORRHE MARKS A MAJOR TURNING POINT IN THE NOVEL ...

It begins with the staging of a homosexual encounter, between Charlus
and Jupien, a tailor, spied on by the narrator. Immediately afterwards,
he goes to the princesse de Guermantes's party, and starts to see
evidence of homosexuality everywhere. The narrator and Swann

discuss jealousy. Swann is dying. The narrator's relationship with Albertine is developing. Odette's salon is gaining prominence. The Dreyfus Affair is coming to an end.

The narrator goes to Balbec for the second time. Although involved with Albertine, he is still on the lookout for other sexual conquests. At Balbec, he suddenly understands that his grandmother is dead, when he happens to repeat one of her actions. His mother has come to resemble the grandmother.

Albertine comes to Balbec. The narrator is undecided about her. One night he sees her dancing with Andrée, and feels excluded. Albertine seems to watch other women as much as he does. He vacillates between indifference and desire as he socializes. Homosexual scandals come to light around them. Charlus meets his great love Morel. Their affair parallels the narrator's with Albertine. The Verdurins have rented a property called La Raspelière on the coast, and have parties there. Albertine and the narrator tour the countryside at speed in a car. The narrator feels low-level, but constant jealousy about Albertine, and tries to disengage himself. Meanwhile Charlus's jealousy about Morel takes on violent qualities. La Raspelière can be reached by means of a little coastal train. Accounts of the trips turn into a series of stories, all of them scandalous.

It is in this train that Albertine reveals to the narrator that she had known Vinteuil's daughter and her lesbian lover. To control the explosion of jealousy this causes, the narrator demands that Albertine come to live with him in Paris. There he will be able to monitor her movements and control her sexuality.

LA PRISONNIÈRE IS THE ACCOUNT OF THIS IMPRISONMENT ...

Jealousy, the narrator's intermittent illness, paralyses him. Albertine manipulates and evades his jealousy. His paralysis and her evasiveness form two mutually reinforcing survival strategies. Bergotte dies.

Charlus is running to seed. His 'vice' has taken control of him, and is terrifying. The Verdurins hold a recital of a lost work by Vinteuil, a Septet. It inspires the narrator. The Verdurins conspire to expel Charlus from their salon, humiliating him in public. Morel is becoming an established violinist. He rejects Charlus. Swann has died, unnoticed.

Returning from the recital, the narrator and Albertine fight. She nearly betrays something unforgivable. They are sad and tender with one another. He anticipates the end of their relationship, through a series of premonitions. He wakes up one morning determined to cut it off. Françoise pre-empts him, with the news that she has already gone.

ALBERTINE DISPARUE (LITERALLY ALBERTINE DISAPPEARED) FOLLOWS THE CONSEQUENCES OF ALBERTINE'S DEPARTURE ...

The narrator, in a panic, has her followed by Saint-Loup, but he fails to persuade her to return. Then suddenly, a telegram announces that she has been killed in a riding accident. A prolonged period of mourning ensues, as the narrator slowly recovers. He describes how he is repeatedly overwhelmed by memories of her, and how these gradually give way to indifference. He even experiences posthumous jealousy, desperately trying to uncover the truth about her sexuality. Mourning is the reversal out of love.

The narrator's article is published in the *Figaro*. Gilberte is finally welcomed into the Guermantes circle, having repudiated her Jewish father, Swann. The narrator goes to Venice with his mother. He receives a telegram, apparently from Albertine – but it is from Gilberte, announcing her marriage to Saint-Loup. But very soon the narrator realizes that he is homosexual, like his uncle Charlus. Saint-Loup has an affair with Morel. The narrator goes to stay with Gilberte at Tansonville, Swann's estate. There he discovers that the two 'ways' unite.

THE FINAL PART OF *A LA RECHERCHE, LE TEMPS RETROUVÉ* ...

Opens at Tansonville. The narrator reads a 'memoir', by the Goncourt brothers (this is one of the most famous of Proust's pastiches). It is an account of a Verdurin dinner. The stilted pomposity of the language is ridiculous, but the narrator sees only his own lack of talent, since his emphasis is psychological and not objective.

We realize later that he has had a breakdown: he returns several times from sanatoria to wartime Paris. The war has turned the French social order upside down. Charlus's degeneration is apparent now from his rampant pro-German ravings, which make him look insane in the context of a war against Germany. Saint-Loup is trying to be sent to the front, to punish himself for being homosexual. The narrator stumbles upon Jupien's male brothel one night, and spies on Charlus being beaten. Even the métro becomes a sexual playground. Saint-Loup is killed. Morel, having been a deserter, becomes a war hero.

After the war, the narrator returns permanently to Paris. He is depressed, unable to start writing. He is invited to a recital at the princesse de Guermantes. Indifferently, he accepts. He meets Charlus on the way. Charlus is a wreck. The past has been turned to dust.

In the courtyard of the Guermantes's property, the narrator accidentally stumbles on an uneven paving stone. An immediate feeling of rapture overwhelms him. It reminds him of eating the *madeleine*. He thinks about Venice. He is shown into the library, to wait for the end of the recital, and is served tea.

The power of involuntary memory

He experiences a series of overwhelming sensations, as he hears the sound of a spoon against a plate, and the rustle of a starched napkin. He has a sudden revelation that these fleeting sensations have the power to bring back the lost past, and that they are a fertile source of creative material. It is not enough to analyse intellectually, and much harder to decipher the untransformed material that is brought back by chance sensations. He notices *François le Champi*, a book his mother used to read to him, and becomes sure that he has found a way to start writing. To transmit this intimate association between sensation and memories of the past, the writer has to translate the impressions into metaphors. The material for the work of literature he wants to write is his own past life, summarized as 'a vocation'. He has done his research without realizing it. He has had an apprenticeship of suffering, but even jealousy has its creative uses. It does not matter what a book is about, it is the subjective way in which it is written that is important – its style.

He goes into the party – and experiences a completely different revelation. His contemporaries are hoary old men and women, still shuffling their anxieties and prejudices about. Madame Verdurin has married the prince de Guermantes and rules the Faubourg Saint-Germain. He is witnessing a competition with death. His own happy fantasy of moments before, the abundant regaining of his past life, has to be juxtaposed against the constant mutation of social structures and other people's individual lives. It is an impossible balancing act and we die of the strain of it. Gilberte presents her daughter, and the narrator sees her as the bodily outcome of all the fragmented moments of his own psychological existence. She is time embodied.

He starts to write, racing against his own death. He wants to construct his novel as a couturier would construct a dress: from an assembly of parts that produces a fluid, malleable whole. At first no one understands his incredible focus. Other people think he wastes time on trivial details, but he thinks of himself as using a telescope rather than a microscope as a viewfinder – his greatest desire is precisely that his novel should unfold over time, but also show time unfolding.

A LA RECHERCHE: THE ROAD MAP
Instead of summarizing this chapter, it might be useful to see the novel spread out like a road map. This means cutting out two dimensions (space and time), leaving us with a flat plan of the novel's plot.

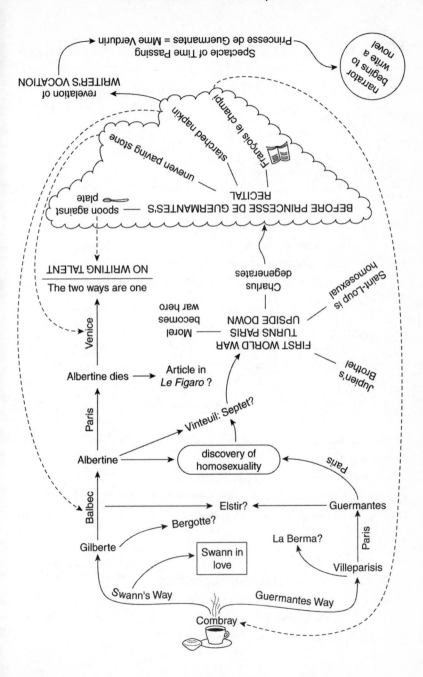

7 Proust's Major Themes & Ideas

CREATIVE INFLUENCES AND LITERARY THEORY IN
A LA RECHERCHE

Proust believed in the novel form as the most flexible, subtle and powerful art form, but announced this only after scrupulous attention to photography, music, painting, sculpture and other people's novels. There is a vast network of references to playwrights, art critics, poets, scientists, and even military strategists, spreading through this novel. All art forms are attempts to represent reality, and so they all develop their own language. Proust was fascinated by the possibilities of so many entirely distinct languages competing to represent objective reality. His obsession with language is a dominant force in *A la recherche*.

Bergotte the writer, Elstir the painter, and Vinteuil the composer are the main fictional representatives of different art forms. One of the ways the book changed as it was being written is that real-life artists were gradually transformed into fictional influences – discovering Wagner's opera was initially supposed to be a turning point in the young narrator's quest for a way to begin writing. In the end, the made-up composer Vinteuil provides this revelation, when the narrator hears his Septet. Even then, it is only once all influences, mentors and guides have been fully abandoned, that the writing of the novel we never read can begin, right at the end of *A la recherche du temps perdu*.

Elstir teaches the young narrator a vital theory of perception in *A l'ombre des jeunes filles en fleurs*. Elstir is a thinly disguised **Impressionist** painter. He represents things in terms of his first impressions of them.

KEYWORD

Impressionism was a concerted attempt to revise stale ways of viewing landscape and figures. It shifted emphasis from the object to the way the object was committed to canvas, thus paving the way for the art movements of the twentieth century, such as Cubism, Dadaism, Surrealism, and Expressionism.

Recognitions and re-inventions

One of the paintings the narrator sees in Elstir's studio is entitled 'Miss Sacripant'. It is a portrait of a boyish woman, in a bowler hat, holding a cigarette, half-dressed as a man. It is her equivocal appearance that seems to fascinate both Elstir and the narrator:

> Along the lines of the face, the latent sex seemed to be on the point of confessing itself to be that of a somewhat boyish girl, then vanished, and reappeared further on with a suggestion rather of an effeminate, vicious and pensive youth, then fled once more and remained elusive. (*A l'ombre des jeunes filles en fleurs*)

This painting turns out to be of Odette. Elstir himself turns out to be the 'Monsieur Biche' of the Verdurin salon. Throughout *A la recherche* we find these recognitions and re-inventions of the characters. Elstir's theory of perception and representation does not only apply to works of art. It may be linked to Proust's overall theory of character, as a multiplying series of identities linked by the passage of time. Just as we judge by first impressions, so those impressions are themselves revised by later incarnations of people we think we know.

Bergotte

Bergotte is a fictional novelist, and so the most proximate kind of artist-mentor for the narrator. At the beginning of the novel he is a near mythical figure, revered as a conduit of truth in writing. Later on, however, he comes to seem more ordinary to the narrator. There are two main scenes involving Bergotte. The first is a lunch party at Odette's, where the narrator sees Bergotte for the first time, and is rather bored by him. Bergotte has a nose like a snailshell, which completely puts the narrator off. His physical reality seems to get in the way of his mastery of prose style. It is not until his death, while at an exhibition of Vermeer's paintings that Bergotte has another major scene. Bergotte is overwhelmed by one apparently insignificant little section of yellow wall in Vermeer's *View of Delft*. "'That's how I ought to have written," he said. "My last books are too dry, I ought to have

Bergotte's nose alarms the narrator.

gone over them with a few layers of colour, made my language precious in itself, like this little patch of yellow wall.'" (*La Prisonnière*).

The novel as superior art form

Proust's discussions of other art forms are ultimately intended to justify the novel form as superior, however much he is at pains to give painting, music, and the relatively late-coming art forms, photography and cinema, a fair hearing. Here is what Proust thought of cinema:

> If reality were indeed a sort of waste product of experience, more or less identical for each one of us, since when we speak of bad weather, a war, a taxi rank, a brightly lit restaurant, a garden full of flowers, everybody knows what we mean, if reality were no more than this, no doubt a sort of cinematograph film of these things would be sufficient and the "style", the "literature" that departed from the simple data that they provide would be superfluous and artificial. (*Le temps retrouvé*)

The fact that you can see an image on a cinema screen drains reality of its complexity, Proust argues. Similarly, we often have to use a dull form of language to make communication simpler, even if it doesn't capture the fullness of our subjective experience. Cinema and everyday language use are too passive for Proust. But writing is pretty demanding. Writing has to overcome its insubstantial, unappealing appearance, and needs the collaboration of readerly imagination in order to have an effect. Writing can only project immaterial visual images onto a mental screen. Reading doesn't happen unless you read. And worst of all, words actually get in the way of transmitting meaning. One of the most important meditations on literary theory occurs at the end of *Le temps retrouvé*, as the narrator waits to be admitted to his final aristocratic party. Perhaps its most crucial maxim is this: 'The function and the task of a writer are those of a translator' (*Le temps retrouvé*).

PROUST'S METAPHORS

The narrator in the novel is constantly shown trying to translate the raw chaos of experience into language. Paradoxically, Proust is stuck with the technical problem of illustrating how these primary experiences felt to his narrator, since his own raw material is language. Proust's solution is to convey the narrator's chaotic childhood impressions by means of metaphor.

Metaphors are technically an attempt to convey an idea by means of substitution. 'My love is a rose' does not mean that I have fallen in love with a rose, but that only the idea of a rose, fragrant and thorny, will do to convey to a third party the quality of my feelings for the person I love.

Fusion and exchange

Proust's metaphors are spectacular – but for a very particular reason. It is not because they are far-fetched, but because they are firmly embedded in the context that is being described. Proust achieves an amazing effect of transposition. Rather than bringing together completely unrelated objects, he will substitute the qualities of one object for another object perhaps geographically close by. This creates the effect of fusion, rather than substitution. When you look at a coastal horizon, you cannot tell where the sea stops and the sky begins. This is what Proust's metaphors are like.

Extracting their common essence

Proust uses metaphors as a rigorous scientific protocol: for him, they are the precipitation, the outcome, of the shared qualities of different things, in the form of language that can be analysed. Here is how Proust himself defines metaphor:

> Truth will be attained by [the writer] only when he takes two different objects, states the connection between them – a connection analogous in the world of art to the unique connection which in the world of science is provided by the law of causality – and encloses them in the necessary links of a well-wrought style; truth – and life too – can be attained by us only when, by comparing a quality common to two sensations, we succeed in extracting their common essence and in reuniting them to each other, liberated from the contingencies of time, within a metaphor.
> (*Le temps retrouvé*)

We can illustrate this using another technical language. Water is built of hydrogen and oxygen molecules, and we express this compound as H_2O. The chemical equation is a metaphor because we can read in it how the different objects used to form it have been combined. H_2O both is and is not water. Metaphors both are and are not the things they seek to describe. They are rich approximations to a reality we cannot achieve purchase on in any other way if we use language to do so.

The two 'ways'

One of the grand, overarching metaphors of *A la recherche* is that of the two ways which are actually one. The two 'ways' or walks that the narrator's family regularly embark on, and which the boy sees as so completely and radically separate from each other, turn out, as we have seen, to meet. The two ways have been one way all along but have been kept apart in the narrator's mind because of a basic misunderstanding. The unification of two apparently different things is a metaphor for the retrieval of the past. It also happens to be a good definition of metaphor itself.

Stories are metaphors

We can take this view of how metaphor works in *A la recherche* to a further level. The bulk of *Combray* turns out to be one huge metaphor, a written thing substituted for the thing itself. The child narrator tells us that he could not express himself as he wanted to, yet the adult narrator, looking back at his childhood self, is putting words in the child's mouth. The whole of Combray (the village) emerges, metaphorically speaking, from a cup of tea. But the whole of *Combray* (the story of the narrator's idyllic childhood) is also a metaphor because it is a substitution. It is an approximation to what the adult narrator now remembers of his childhood. What we read are still the edited highlights and not the whole story. We can only talk about our remembered past in metaphorical terms: the past is a compound of memory and language. The past is what we can no longer possess.

Metaphors stitch together unusual qualities in Proust's universe, creating new perceptions. This intricate internal stitching is working at all times to create a much larger through-composed entity. Proust's metaphors work hard for him at a local level, in the telling of a story. They also have an impact on the overall conception of *A la recherche*. It is one of the ways in which the novel hangs together as one work, rather than being a series of disparate stories.

PROUST THE ANTHROPOLOGIST

Third Republic aristocrats

Proust writes a great deal about Third Republic aristocrats, unearthing their rituals and assessing their kinship structures. He considers the great arguments about inherited versus learnt characteristics, that are returning today in the form of the genetics debate.

Snobbery and exclusion

Looking back towards *Combray*, we can see immediately that this theme is inaugurated and orchestrated by the division of the two 'ways' (one organized around sexual memories, the other around social memories). It is also given dramatic form in the shape of characters like Legrandin. He pops up throughout the novel, anxious to conceal his burning social pretensions. The complex posturing that pretentiousness entails occupies a huge amount of Proust's story and preoccupies all the characters to a greater or lesser degree, with the exception of the narrator's beloved grandmother, who seems the only person unaffected by social niceties, and motivated solely by doting love. *Un Amour de Swann* focuses as much on the question of social exclusion and exclusivity as it does on jealous desire. The Verdurins' 'petit clan', and their envious rejection of the *ennuyeux* (salons that exclude the Verdurins) is a principal source of comedy in the novel.

Proust is very interested in case studies of particular characters. One of these is Norpois, a diplomat who, like Swann, visits the narrator's family, and also moves in aristocratic circles. Norpois is a manipulator of language, and so dangerously similar to a writer. The narrator examines Norpois and characters like him minutely, trying to understand the difference between using language to contain and control, and using language to express and explain. Norpois is the quintessential smooth talker. As with Legrandin, it is clear that we are meant to think Norpois is an idiot, but it is crucial to see *how* Proust achieves this result. Both Norpois and Legrandin seek to maintain their status by excluding those whose manners or speech do not replicate the dominant modes and manners.

Exclusion is founded on ritual

Le Côté de Guermantes and large parts of *Sodome et Gomorrhe* are given over to Proust's endless revisitation of the self-regulating rituals on which exclusive social practice is founded, as his narrator goes to theatre, opera, salons, parties, recitals, and dinners. There are a number of set-piece party scenes in the novel through which Proust's narrator steps in rank order. He gradually infiltrates the very highest Faubourg Saint-Germain echelons. This aligns the narrator of *A la recherche* with all the best great nineteenth-century Realist novels' protagonists. A common plot driver for the Realist genre was the working out of social ambitions by the young ingénu, who walks the tightrope of preserving his personal and intellectual integrity while somehow making off with all the worldly prizes.

Proust's critique of complicity

There is an important difference between Balzac, Stendhal, or Flaubert, the three most famous nineteenth-century French Realist novelists, and Proust, a difference which marks Proust out as a twentieth-century writer. While the first three do not see genuine conflict of interests between inhabiting an environment and criticizing it, Proust takes very seriously the idea of *complicity*. The narrator's moral outrage at the empty gestures and navel-gazing of the aristocrats among whom he circulates is not staged through polemic, but modified by an awareness of his own involvement in what he observes – the televisual analogy would be a fly-on-the-wall documentary.

Proust and anti-semitism

He often focuses his critique of snobbery through the lens of the Dreyfus Affair. Although the narrator is not Jewish, Swann, Bloch and many other characters are. Proust documents how the Dreyfus Affair disrupted traditional French allegiances. Intellectuals from the left and right, from the aristocracy and the bourgeoisie, were pro-Dreyfus. He also shows that while political crises hold the mirror to societies, they are also opportunities for exploitation, and their resolution is never permanent.

The most famous Proustian anecdote about aristocratic indifference links up with his ethical analysis. It is the scene where Swann humbly announces his impending death to the duc and duchesse de Guermantes, who, late for a party, dismiss his news as neurosis, and rush off. Minutes later, they are back. The duchesse's shoes do not match her dress, and she needs to change them. Swann the assimilated Jew does not assert his own needs, because his acceptability relies on aristocratic benevolence, which may be withdrawn at any time.

An anthropologist not an apologist

Proust is often accused of being a snob himself, but this is to shoot the messenger. He is an anthropologist rather than an apologist. Proust knows only too well that a critic can become a courtier or a mandarin at a moment's notice. This points to a further important reason why so much of the book is devoted to the study of name-dropping and social climbing. Proust is at all times trying to assess the worth and status of literature itself.

One of the big questions of *A la recherche* is whether art is better than and different from 'life', or whether it serves only as a kind of decorative ornament. There is a surprising link between parties and novels. Literature takes place in the form of written language. Parties take place in the form of spoken language. Parties, like novels, need form, structure and content. They are full of characters competing to tell the best stories, to be the narrators of their own importance – to justify themselves through the exclusion of rivals. Novels are, by definition, equally full of competing narratives. There is an anxiety that underpins the narrator's progress through salon society. We can call it a kind of separation anxiety. The narrator's two central concerns are: (i) to work out what he might put into a novel; and (ii) to maintain social and psychological integrity. If the material that goes into the novel is about worthlessness, then to what extent does that render the novel itself worthless? How could a vantage point be found from which to judge this? Proust is not alone in this anxiety. Confessional novels, such as Helen Fielding's *Bridget Jones's Diary* are founded on this tension.

PROUSTIAN PSYCHOLOGY

Proust is a psychologist who never read Freud. Nevertheless, he is a vital analyst of how our minds function. It is Proust's special achievement to have demonstrated just how closely the areas that we think of as separate spheres of mental activity, like 'intellect', 'memory', 'desire', 'anxiety', 'planning', are interconnected, and how closely meshed thought and feeling are.

Proustian memory.

Memory

Proust wrote a great deal about the effects of habit on us. Habit is both positive and negative. Our habitual actions may deaden our thought processes – but they also help us get over the anxiety of new situations. We form habits through repeating actions without thinking. Habit needs mechanical memory to block out emotional memory.

Proust made a distinction between two kinds of memory: voluntary and involuntary. What we try to remember is good for everyday usage; what we try to remember of our past lives is also a pretty good shorthand, telling us basic things about who we are and were. But it is only when we can compare this to *involuntary* memory that we see how impoverished and distorted habitual recall is. It is involuntary recall which supplies lost epochs intact. True involuntary remembrance is a technically tricky mechanism to provoke, since it only happens by chance. Proust contrasts traumatic memory with the intensely stimulating pain of reliving past pleasure. These memories are triggered through sensory experiences of sounds or tastes or smells. They bypass our higher brain function to set off the far more strongly felt emotions that accompanied an event in the past. When people talk about feeling the loss of a beloved, or suddenly reliving a beautiful day, a fabulous painting, or a thrilling football match, they are describing what Proust meant by involuntary memory. Definitions of memory were not, however, Proust's main purpose. He was trying to write down what it feels like to possess the ability to remember in the first place.

Association

A la recherche demonstrates two main kinds of investigative analysis – Proust pursues unusual connections but he also focuses almost obsessively on particular events or characteristics which fascinate him.

One way to look at *A la recherche* is to compare the way it works to using the World Wide Web. Everything in this long novel – ideas, characters, themes, stories – can connect up with everything else. Making connections is not a passive process. Although information is available 'on' the Web, you still have to search for it, often by pursuing likely associations. In *A l'ombre des jeunes filles en fleurs*, the narrator goes to a restaurant at the coastal resort of Balbec, with his friend Saint-Loup. The narrator is slightly drunk, and the restaurant seems to spin as though it were a constellation of stars. When the narrator sees that bustling restaurants are like planetary activity, an associative connection is being made.

Alternatively, we can think about *A la recherche* in terms of hypertext. You can supplement basic information by following up links into sources of more complex detail. When Swann tries to find out whether Odette is lying to him, the obsessive focus of his jealous imagination reveals more and more material to investigate. Proust uses metaphor as scientific modelling equipment with which to build hypotheses about the world. And he shows that emotions we usually deny, like jealousy, are vital investigative tools which enable us to probe and pursue questions we need to research. Unfortunately, jealousy has a design

Proustian hypertext.

flaw, which is its potential to assume the worst possible interpretation of its object's behaviour from the outset, and before actually analysing the available data.

Triggering our memories

As you read *A la recherche* you may gradually become aware that your own mind is making amazing associations. Events or sensations forgotten from your life may suddenly reappear to you in technicolor. Humans can remember things through conscious recall, but we also remember through chance association. Our memories are triggered. These memories may reappear as single images, or as a series of images. They may stand for a long period of time. Or they may represent a single event of life-affecting importance to us. In a way, Proust argued, we are what we forget. What we forget does not disappear. It becomes intricately embedded in the way we see ourselves, and the rest of the world. Proust dramatizes how the process of mourning is one of the ways in which we 'lose' time. But it is a vital loss. Mourning allows us to forget pain, guilt and ambivalence. Without forgetting, we would not be able to remember anything, because we would be mad.

Voluntary and involuntary memory.

Think about situations in which you feel insecure and unhappy. These situations often share similarities. Perhaps you are always nervous in restaurants. Or you find that you want to hit people who pay you compliments. Or you are consumed with giggles whenever you see a bare ankle. For Proust, the key to understanding this insecurity lies in unravelling all the unconscious associations you may have with particular situations. Proust's demonstration that our brain function is intermittent rather than continuous, a space of triggered signals and not a storehouse, tallies with what we know about brain activity. Proust's achievement is to model this associative, intermittent functioning in narrative form.

Sexuality

> Gomorrah was dispersed to the four corners of the earth.
>
> (*La Prisonnière*)

Proust argued passionately for the idea that human sexuality manifests itself in a huge range of ways. He is one of the great analysts of male and female heterosexuality and homosexuality – and their discontents. He is fascinated by the connections we make between sexuality and morality. He demonstrates continually that human sexuality underpins and drives every other part of the psyche. Our desires control our everyday as well as our long range actions. They cause us to make fools of ourselves, lie, suffer maddening jealousy, betray our best friends. Worst of all, they cause us to seek to destroy the very thing we love, in trying to possess it completely.

Sexual desire, morality and art

Justifying what art is worth is a major driving force in *A la recherche*, and is closely connected to Proust's exploration of morality and sexual desire. The narrator spies on a scene of lesbian sadism while walking near Swann's estate one evening, and this sets up an important development much later, in *La Prisonnière*. One of the women is the daughter of the musician, Vinteuil. The narrator watches Vinteuil's daughter and her lesbian lover desecrating the memory of the composer father by mocking his photograph. Vinteuil composes an unperformed Septet, which the daughter's lover unearths after his death, and transcribes from a practically illegible scrawl, so that it can be published. It is when the narrator hears the Septet, much later in the novel, that his dreams of being a writer are revived. He starts to believe again that art is something vitally different from life, and not just a decorative fringe benefit. In *A la recherche*, the narrator uses the example of the loving transcription to justify the apparent 'wickedness' of Vinteuil's daughter and her lesbian partner (for wickedness in Proust, read homosexuality): the lover's remorse is what prompts her to ensure his immortality as a composer.

Forensic sexual jealousy

At other points, however, he is very far from indulging female homosexuality. The spectre of Albertine's possible lesbianism hounds the narrator as his jealousy amplifies. We never discover for sure whether or not she has had lesbian encounters. Instead, the narrator's forensic suspicion powers the monstrous creation that is *La Prisonnière*, a narrative experiment in depicting compulsion that has never been matched. The pursuit of fugitive desire is one of the great themes of this novel, but the difference between *A la recherche* and other accounts of desire is the relentless elaboration of the multiple perspectives jealousy opens up, and the elevation of jealousy into a scientific tool and methodology. Proust manages to imply that not to be jealous is to be somehow emotionally deficient.

Homosexuality and digression

Proust's famously digressive sentences incorporate startling new writing about sexuality, especially homosexuality, tucked away into corners of the narrative. The opening of *Sodome et Gomorrhe* returns to the form that Proust abandoned when he began *A la recherche*: the essay. However it is not a pure essay, but a hybrid. The narrative moves between plot action and a theoretical discussion. The beginning of *Sodome et Gomorrhe* is itself a deviation from the plot, a separate chapter. Proust stages a homosexual encounter, between Charlus and Jupien, a tailor (who we later see running a male brothel during the First World War). The story of how this encounter takes place is intercut with another story. The narrator is spying on the Baron, but simultaneously looking to see whether a bee will pollinate an orchid in the courtyard his family shares with the Guermantes family. The intercutting is exploited to set up an analogy between homosexuality in humans and self-fertilization in plants. Proust argues that occasional self-fertilization can put right genetic deviation, which might otherwise take hold in a given species. Deviation, in Proust's vision, corrects for deviation.

André Gide, another dominant voice in French literature, criticized Proust for such a coy, over-anxious approach to the subject of homosexuality. This criticism seems pretty unwarranted. Proust is one of the first writers to discuss the psychology of homosexuality, rather than offer an allegory for it, as Oscar Wilde had done. Evidence of male and female homosexuality spreads like wildfire throughout the second half of the novel. Proust treats it both as a vital explanatory device for social cohesion, and as a disruptive, vicious breach of normative morals. Proust's is one of the most exhaustive investigations of human pleasure, and the shifting moral prescriptions we use to contain it, ever to have been written.

Multiple Selves

Proust runs the risk of being labelled a self-obsessed neurotic in order to give shape to a radically unsettling theory of selfhood. He argues that we are not one self, but many. He tries to show that we don't experience ourselves as single individuals, but as different people, with different identities, over the course of our lives. This is because humans are extraordinarily adaptable, malleable creatures, able to absorb and react to extreme change, through the deceptively simple expedient of thinking about it. One major advantage of this theory is that it acknowledges the intense series of *non sequiturs* that career through our minds all the time, as we process changes in external circumstances.

For most practical purposes, unfortunately, we have to iron out these bubbling self-contradictions in favour of an appearance of balanced, amenable, controlled reciprocity. Yet even smoothing over internal contradictions has something to tell us about self-preservation. Proust demonstrates on a grand scale the sheer effort of will that is demanded by everyday suffering, or writing novels, or conducting jealous love affairs, or staying sane under the pressures of war.

There are seemingly endless ways in which we are not ever actually ourselves. Proust shows us this divisibility and multiplication of ourselves and other people from internal and external vantage points.

Early on in the novel, he establishes the most basic way in which we are all at least double: 'our social personality is a creation of the thoughts of other people' (*Du côté de chez Swann*). There is no way for us ever to be fully ourselves because other people make assumptions about us.

He doesn't just discuss social appearance versus personal reality, however. He is at pains to show how we experience *ourselves* differently over time. Here are some examples:

* Jealousy acts like an atomizer, blasting the lover and the beloved into fragmentary images of themselves: '[Swann] was jealous, now, of that other self whom she had loved' (*Un Amour de Swann*). Swann is jealous of himself.

* Madame Verdurin ends up married to the prince de Guermantes, and transforms herself from a pretentious inverted snob into an aristocrat.

* Charlus, Saint-Loup, and countless other men in the novel undergo complete sexual transformation.

* The bewitching cluster of young girls at Balbec functions like a swarm of athletic bees, as a homogeneous whole, until the narrator homes in on Albertine.

* Albertine then breaks down into a series of different perspectives, as her identity subdivides under the glaring intensity of the narrator's obsession.

* And finally, after Albertine runs away we find some of the most compelling analyses for this theory of multiple personalities, in the mourning for lost love:

    At every moment, there was one more of those innumerable and humble "selves" that compose our personality which was still unaware of Albertine's departure and must be informed of it. (*Albertine disparue*)

PROUST THE MORALIST

We live in an era which is often defined as being politically and culturally aligned with the individual perspective. As we live more and more outside family or community structures, our personal identities become the guarantors, even the models, for good living. Proust not only understood this first, and wrote about it better than anyone else. He also considered all the ethical dangers of the seductive subjective perspective.

The very foundation and structure of *A la recherche du temps perdu* demonstrates this focus on ethical danger. By writing in the first person voice, but by deliberately writing fiction and not autobiography, Proust is issuing a direct challenge to us, his readers. He demands that we consider what it is we are doing whenever we start sentences with 'I hope', or 'I hate'. We are trapped by ourselves as much as liberated by our thoughts. There is a constant tension in Proust's writing between the desire to see the world from one point of view, and building multiple perspectives which will enable the narrator to avoid believing just one interpretation of the world.

Recognizing this tension is absolutely vital to understanding why Proust is a great writer and not just a chronicler of his own life and the lives of his friends. It is his determined effort to keep asking difficult questions about the interconnections between psychological and moral motivation which also keeps his book alive and constantly mobile. Françoise the servant kills a chicken and scolds it for not dying easily. Madame Verdurin excommunicates the pitiful Saniette and the blustering, childlike Charlus from her personal fiefdom, in order to gratify her own insecurities. The narrator himself pursues the fugitive sexuality of his lover Albertine until, in possessing her entirely, his obsession crushes her vitality. Proust is not content to say that these actions are wrong, he wants to understand why they are pleasurable – and therefore likely to go on happening.

AN ANALYSIS OF TIME

An hour is not merely an hour, it is a vase full of scents and sounds and projects and climates, and what we call reality is a certain connection between these immediate sensations and the memories which envelop us simultaneously with them. (*Le temps retrouvé*)

Proust had double vision.

Proust's vision of the world has been called 'binocular'. He has, effectively, double vision. He sees things, people and events from the inside out and the outside in. He sees things proceeding in a circular not linear fashion. Love affairs are repetitions of earlier ones – the pattern simply repeats, amplifies and intensifies. The way each of us loves does not change once it is fully formed, it just comes round again and again. Social circles merely change their participants, but not their essential form. Time – or rather, the way we experience time – doesn't pass in a straight line, since there isn't actually a way of separating time from our sense of being alive. We just need to think there is, or else we could never catch trains or meet friends. The way we experience time, Proust demonstrates, is both as something that moves and as something that stays the same. And the easiest way to think about this is with a metaphor: if we imagine cooking dehydrated food, we can easily see that it both changes (given some water it seems a lot more appetizing) and stays the same (it was edible in the first place). Repetition and variation turn out to be inextricably connected.

A la recherche du temps perdu tries to explain the relationship between two kinds of time. We can call them *punctuality* and *duration*. Punctuality means the kind of time we need to live in organized communities, to catch trains, meet each other, remember anniversaries and so on. 'Let's meet at 2.45' expresses our reliance on punctuality as a way of cutting up time. Duration, on the other hand, refers to the way experiences connect up with one another, in sequences which we can reconstruct. 'Last year I was so unhappy' expresses an attempt to convey an experience taking place over a period of time. 'The war lasted for four years' is not an expression of duration, but a way of cutting up time into chunks. 'We thought the war would never end', on the other hand, tells us something about what the experience of war time was like. 'Punctuality' implies social contracts, duty, the obligation to suppress personal experience in favour of the social good. 'Duration' implies personal experience as well as the attempt to record, retrieve and analyse it.

Proust is most famous for being an analyst of time past, or of wasting time. But this is just the tip of the Proustian iceberg. Time is, of course, treated as straightforwardly chronological, asserting its effects on us all. But it is also, and this is Proust's special genius, treated as an intricately layered, circular and repetitive set of experiences. He has offered us an extensive array of tools with which to model our own mental apparatus, and our own constantly fluctuating consciousness, passing through time. And this makes him an extraordinarily important figure in our overall understanding of cultural and temporal metamorphosis. He is not a transitory writer of ephemera, but one of the most sophisticated and significant analysts of *change* ever to have existed.

✳ ✳ ✳ ✳*SUMMARY*✳ ✳ ✳ ✳

- Proust fictionalized external influences from other art forms.

- He uses metaphor as a scientific tool.

- He is an anthropologist of the aristocracy, not an apologist for snobbery.

- His psychological range includes:
  – analysis of forgetting and associative recall
  – spectrum of sexualities
  – theory of multiple selves.

- He analyses the dangers of subjectivity: the tension between a subjective perspective and the denial of other people.

- He analyses time non-chronologically, as duration.

Modern Critical Approaches

A work in which there are theories is like an object which still has its price-tag on it. (Le temps retrouvé)

There are as many ways to read as there are readers of literature. But since around 1915–16, when Ferdinand de Saussure, an expert in linguistics, was developing a new theory of how language worked, literary criticism has developed many new approaches to reading, each with its own method and theory behind it. This section of the *Beginner's Guide* introduces what a deconstructive way of reading *A la recherche* entails; how a feminist might interpret this novel; and what insights a theory such as psychoanalysis can offer. It is vital to remember that these are only approaches, never truths about *A la recherche*. The good thing about modern literary criticism is that it can both enhance our analytical abilities and enable us to make connections between individual authors and other parts of human existence. The downside of literary criticism is that it is always in danger of seeming dogmatic or closed.

A BRIEF INTRODUCTION TO MODERN CRITICAL THEORIES

We will be looking at one particular passage from *Albertine disparue* in order to introduce deconstructionist, feminist and psychoanalytical readings. The passage comes from late in *A la recherche*. It describes a moment when, after Albertine's death, the narrator has gone with his mother to Venice. There he receives a telegram. Here is the passage:

One evening, however, an incident occurred of such a nature that it seemed as though my love must revive. No sooner had our gondola stopped at the hotel steps than the porter handed me a telegram which the messenger had already brought three times to the hotel, for owing to the inaccurate rendering of the addressee's name (which I recognized nevertheless, through the corruptions introduced by the Italian clerks, as my own) the post office required a signed receipt certifying that the telegram was indeed for me. I opened it as soon as I was in my room, and, glancing through the message which was filled with inaccurately transmitted words, managed nevertheless to make out: "My dear friend, you think me dead, forgive me, I am quite alive, I long to see you, talk about marriage, when do you return? Affectionately. Albertine." Then there occurred in me in reverse order a process parallel to that which had occurred in the case of my grandmother. When I had learned the fact of my grandmother's death, I had not at first felt any grief. And I had been really grieved by her death only when certain involuntary memories had brought her alive again for me. Now that Albertine no longer lived for me in my thoughts, the news that she was alive did not cause me the joy that I might have expected. Albertine had been no more to me than a bundle of thoughts, and she had survived her physical death so long as those thoughts were alive in me; on the other hand, now that those thoughts were dead, Albertine did not rise again for me with the resurrection of her body.

(Albertine disparue)

Having equipped ourselves with a specific passage from *A La Recherche*, it might be useful to recap the history of modern critical theory, albeit in potted form. Then we can look at specific instances of deconstructive, feminist and psychoanalytic interpretation.

SAUSSURE AND A THEORY OF LANGUAGE

Saussure proposed that a language is a system of **signs**. He suggested that language is made up of signs having only an arbitrary relationship with the things to which they refer. Yet the link between **signifier** and **signified** is based on convention, nothing more binding. Language users rely on a contract of agreed use in order to make themselves understood and to understand.

KEYWORD

Saussure argued that a sign is made up of a signifier (word) and a signified (object), and these are not linked by any natural resemblance. The sign 'chair' is made up of the letters C-H-A-I-R (the **signifier**) together with the object it designates (a four-legged thing to sit on – the signified).

Languages are individual systems of concepts. These concepts are identified as much through their differences from each other as they are by convention. A chair is a chair because it is *not* a sofa or a stool – or a *chaise*.

The implications of Saussurian linguistics are huge. Once we look at language in this way, differences between, for example, French and English, start to seem worthy of close attention rather than simply quaint or charming. If the words we use are only arbitrarily tied to the things they describe, then language systems must be playing a major part in organizing the way we understand our environment, experience, and identities. French is not just different from English, the two different languages are actually structuring how people think about themselves in ways that are fundamentally untranslatable.

Language systems become the privileged way into understanding one's own culture or a foreign culture, but are simultaneously treacherous and unstable. Saussure was proposing a theory of language which suggested that we do not fully control what comes out of our mouths, that language may in some sense control us, and that languages are systems that work by exclusion. He was hinting that things only exist in language by virtue of what they are not.

FROM STRUCTURALISM TO POST-STRUCTURALISM

Saussure's thinking led on to an enormous amount of study in the twentieth century, and allowed whole new fields of enquiry to gain credibility. Literary criticism, history, political theory, architecture, feminism, anthropology, psychoanalysis, among other areas of research, all owe substantial debts to his view of how powerful and yet unstable language is.

KEYWORDS

Semiotics The science of signs or grammar.

Structuralism Structuralist thinkers established semiotics to explain the underlying structures of phenomena as diverse as the family, fashion, or literary texts.

Literary criticism worldwide went through many permutations in the last century. One of the most notorious was labelled structuralism.

Roland Barthes and structuralism

One of the most famous of the critics loosely grouped by the term structuralism was Roland Barthes, who published the essay *The Death of the Author* in 1968. This argued that readers construct the meanings of texts, rather than finding those meanings spelt out for them by the authors of texts. In 1970 Barthes also produced *S/Z*, the classic structuralist reading of the Balzac novella, *Sarrasine*. He cut up the text into 561 chunks, then offered readings of these *lexies*, together with a running commentary on his unfolding method. It offers us five codes around and through which stories are organized: codes representing actions, the plot or quest of the story, characterization, themes or symbols, and cultural reference in which the story is embedded. Barthes was not the only critic to come up with a textual mark-up system, but his remains the most successful.

Structuralism itself gave way to fragmented modifications and new theories at the end of the 1960s, as critics saw a major flaw in how semiotics was conceived. Barthes marked the crucial shift of emphasis which has characterized post-structural ways of thinking. What was becoming clearer was that there was no way to be objective about criticism – not because literary criticism is just personal opinion, but because there was no place in the language system that was constructing us from which to formulate an objective critique. What was needed was an account of subjectivity, and an account of the instability of language, which could move more easily between language as a system and language as it is used in writing books, making television programmes, and in everyday relationships. The attempt to find a science of signs diversified into many new theories about the relationship between language and reality.

Post-structuralism is a term that designates a broad range of theoretical approaches to texts, films, buildings, politics, and so forth, that developed from the 1970s onwards. Among these approaches we can name deconstruction, feminism, and psychoanalysis. Others are marxism, post-colonialism, new historicism and queer theory. Post-structuralist thinkers do not form a coherent school of thought. Rather they have in common a suspicion of the way theories become tangled up in what they seek to explain. Feminists can't just do away with men or babies. Psychoanalysts are just as likely to suffer from neurosis as their analysands. Marxism cannot account satisfactorily for post-revolutionary suffering, for evolutionary inequality, and for greed.

Post-structuralists are also linked through a recognition that phenomena such as texts, other people, and the weather, don't behave according to the structures that are supposed to describe them. Basically, there's still no way to define a novel, just as there's still no cure for the common cold. Post-structuralists are suspicious of closed systems and structures, hierarchies and total, definitive explanations. They criticize how power is hidden and unevenly distributed; they inspect apparently clear definitions of knowledge for fudging; and they see our personal identity as something that has been constructed by influences upon us, and our own performance of identity. Identity, for post-structuralists, is not something we are born with. Post-structuralist readings are also aware of the complicity operating between people, who think they are autonomous individuals, and organizations, such as multi-national corporations, state apparatuses, education systems, the family, and the ecosystem.

WHAT IS DECONSTRUCTION?

Deconstruction is one of the strands of post-structuralism. Deconstructionists start from the assumption that they cannot assume a word or sentence will have one meaning, since the same word can have many different meanings. To de-construct means to undo. This should not be taken to mean that a deconstructive reading of a novel is destructive. A deconstructive reading picks up terms which are carrying assertive

> **KEYWORD**
>
> Deconstruction is a way of analysing language. Rather than seeing language as conveying fixed meanings, a decon-structionist questions whether those meanings are actually so certain.

weight in texts, i.e. words which are being used to guarantee the credibility of a text. These words are then teased out for the meanings they exclude.

These excluded meanings exert a silenced but definite pressure which undoes what the argument apparently says transparently and sincerely. A deconstructionist would look at the phrase 'This policy is safe as houses' and question whether domestic spaces are safe or dangerous.

Deconstruction is not a rulebook for close reading or practical criticism. It is, at its most ambitious, an ongoing project to question the assumptions that people in the Western world have traditionally made about appearance and reality. Jacques Derrida, the philosopher and critic, argues, for example, that speech has been privileged over writing by philosophers. Speech is seen as being somehow more 'direct', while writing is a deferral and a substitution for the pure 'presence' of someone speaking without mediation. Writing *supplements* speech. A *supplement*, however, is an addition that *completes* a structure – like the colour supplement in the Sunday newspapers. Speech is dependent on the existence of writing to be defined as 'more direct' than writing. This shows us that there is no 'safe place' from which to talk about language objectively.

WHAT IS A DECONSTRUCTIVE READING OF *A LA RECHERCHE*?

Ever since Proust first published *A la recherche*, people have been trying to guess the identities of the characters he portrays. Because it is written in the first person, and the past tense, confusion with the genre of autobiography is impossible to avoid – especially because the narrator is named at several points in the book as Marcel. Since post-structuralist ideas came to prominence after the 1960s, autobiography has attracted a great deal of interest. Autobiography relies on two things: the author's sincerity and the reader's trust. But if language is not a transparent purveyor of fixed and stable meanings, then an autobiographical text will not be fully under the control of its author, which also calls into question the means needed to construct the text (the reliability of the author's memory and sources, for example). Proust's agile hopping between fiction and fact is already an exercise in deconstruction. In fact deconstructionists can only say that this proves their point. Texts deconstruct themselves. They contain contradictory logics.

If this were the conclusion of all deconstructive readings, however, post-structuralism would hardly have caught on as it has. So what can deconstructive reading do? Let us reconsider our passage from *Albertine disparue*.

On the face of it, Albertine seems to write from the dead in this passage. In fact later, the telegram turns out to be from Gilberte, the narrator's first girlfriend, now married to Saint-Loup. The narrator misreads the signature, but it is an act of misreading which enables him to liberate himself from the state of mourning, an error that conceals a correction.

The telegram is not the only key term in this passage. Another striking phrase is the one the narrator uses to describe Albertine: a 'bundle of thoughts'. As an insubstantial bundle of thoughts ('un faisceau de pensées' in the French), an immaterial version of Albertine had survived Albertine's physical death to live on in the narrator's mind. This word 'faisceau' is not as benign as it seems. The narrator could have talked of 'un fagot de pensées', the old French term for bundle. A *faisceau* comes from the Latin *fascis*, a bundle of rods bound up with an axe in the middle, its blade projecting. It is a symbol for power, and it is from *fascis* that we derive the term *fascism*. The narrator has adopted Roman law in his language, adopted its controlling ideology as his own mental containment strategy for dead Albertine. Her resurrection would upset his careful patrolling possession of her. While she is dead, he can love her unconditionally. If she is alive, all pretence at love falls apart into the desperate agony of jealousy. Her resurrection is an insurrection, his Venetian empire is threatened by it.

This is a deconstructive reading of the text. The bundled meanings of key words in it are undone, to show how the text is working, fascistically, to cover up the traces of unspeakable meanings, meanings that are absent from the surface, but whose ghostly presences are constructing its power. A deconstructive reading shows where power lies.

WHAT IS FEMINIST LITERARY CRITICISM?

Feminist criticism paralleled the worldwide twentieth-century social movements seeking to improve the conditions under which women live. It was well established in university writing and teaching by the 1960s. It offers alternative readings of male-authored work in many different spheres, showing how assumptions that men dominate and rule societies are contrived rather than natural.

> **KEYWORD**
>
> Feminist criticism questions prejudices parading themselves as truths about the nature of femininity, embedded in everyday speech, political rhetoric, and action. It seeks to retrieve the work (intellectual, artistic, scientific) of women which has been lost to view or appropriated by others.

Broadly speaking, the feminist literary critical world divides into two streams. One strand is formed by the Anglo-American feminists, who tend to focus their attention on social parity, and the recognition of women's work, in all its forms. The other strand is broadly known as French or Continental feminism, and has tended to explore the possibilities of what is called 'écriture féminine', a specifically feminine form of writing. Continental feminism has been more engaged with post-Romantic philosophy and psychoanalytic theory.

With the gains of political feminism, a third wave of feminists has come to prominence, who are now exploring the way masculinity has also been constructed. These feminists question whether the needs of both men and women are fully articulated and met through oppositional debate.

It is much clearer now that feminism has been extremely successful in challenging misogynist assumptions in well developed democracies and open economies. Millions of women, however, still endure oppression in fundamentalist states and under-developed economies. There are now multiple feminisms united by a common refusal of misogyny, but each exploring the needs of specific groups of women living in deprived or embattled conditions.

WHAT IS A FEMINIST READING OF *A LA RECHERCHE*?

You might wonder how this highly politicized mode of thinking can be applied to Proust. In general terms, Proust is considered in two ways by feminists. He is often shown to be a misogynist writer, who portrays the narrator's jealous imprisonment of Albertine as a morally acceptable, if painful, form of romantic attachment. Indeed Albertine is often read as a thinly disguised version of Agostinelli, Proust's chauffeur, who died in 1914. But this kind of transposition does not really do justice to Proust's portrayal of femininity. He shows both femininity and masculinity to be complex, nuanced, and provisional modes of being, and in this can be considered a post-modernist before his time. While clearly at times exploiting the conventional representations of women available at the turn of the last century, as he does in portraying homosexuality, Proust also challenges stereotyping, with the subtlety of his characterization.

Looking at the same passage from *A la recherche* quoted above, we can see various areas that might be given a feminist critique. The clearest characteristic of Albertine's seems to be her ambiguous availability. Is she or is she not waiting for the narrator back home? If we consider the assumptions on which this rests: that women are difficult if they are less than fully available to men; that their demands are inopportune, untrustworthy, and threatening; that they lurk in domestic spaces, we can see that Albertine has been framed up.

There is another, more disturbing, reading to be made from this passage. The narrator analyses his feelings by way of a comparison with his feelings about another woman, his grandmother. Femininity emerges from this passage not only as positive or negative availability, but also as a closed system of relational comparisons. Albertine emerges as the object of the narrator's subjective interpretation, part of a series of interchangeable objects, not a subject in her own right.

WHAT IS PSYCHOANALYTIC LITERARY CRITICISM?

KEYWORD

Psychoanalytic criticism Criticism which applies the theories of Sigmund Freud to textual analysis and in particular looks at the unconscious motivations of both authors and characters.

Psychoanalysis seeks to cure neurosis. It does so through an analysis of associations made during therapeutic sessions. It has a well developed theoretical framework. Psychological conflicts unresolved during childhood are repressed as the child gets older. They manifest themselves in later life, either as harmless unconscious slips of the tongue, or in dreams, or in disturbed behaviour. These early conflicts are to do with desires that are frustrated. The objects of these desires are usually the child's parents, who are also the source of the frustration. Psychoanalysis is a two-way, dynamic, and interactive series of encounters between an analyst who has undergone therapy, and an analysand who is trying to resolve psychological problems.

Psychoanalytic Criticism

With the developing understanding that psychological material is not merely projected by the analysand onto the analyst in what is termed 'transference', but is also transmitted by the analyst to the analysand under the sway of 'countertransference', psychoanalytic literary criticism has become much more subtle and open-ended. The main movement within the field has been away from the attempt to produce 'finished' ('cured') readings of novels, plays and films, towards indeterminate readings, which take their cue from the work of Jacques Lacan, a charismatic and complex theorist.

Psychoanalytic criticism has the advantage of focusing our attention on the deficiencies of memory, and the profoundly uncontrollable nature of speech, as well as drawing our attention to the monstrously egotistical components of our psychosexual identities.

WHAT IS A PSYCHOANALYTIC READING OF *A LA RECHERCHE*?

Psychoanalytic literary criticism usually looks for hidden, unexpressed conflicts in texts, and often finds them in uncanny moments, which resist interpretation, seeming to contain multiple meanings. 'Uncanny' comes from the German *unheimlich*, which literally means 'un-home-like'. Looking once again at the passage we have been considering, Albertine's return from the dead, asking when the narrator will return home, to the place where the telegram must have come from, is uncanny.

Yet the translated telegram, a kind of written ghost of Albertine's ambiguous presence, half-alive, semi-legible, is not what is most foreign and strange about this passage. What is uncanny about Proust's text is the way the narrator is so quick to domesticate his reaction to the telegram through self-exposure. He controls his feelings by exposing them. His response bypasses any surprise at the oddity of the telegram, any rational attempt to find out where it came from or if he has understood it properly. The telegram from the supposedly dead Albertine immediately functions as an opportunity to marshal and parade the narrator's anxieties. In this first-person text, we find the narrator quite at home with his own analysis, deliberately feeding external data into the dynamic conflicts which both drive and obstruct his intellectual progress towards writing a novel. He himself asserts that he feels things the wrong way round – he did not feel grief for his grandmother's death until he had imagined her as alive. Albertine's ambiguous state is immediately appropriated, and inverted to become the narrator's ambivalent feelings towards her. Self-analysis is like a cuckoo, making its home in another bird's nest – it usurps the expression of emotion felt towards another.

✳ ✳ ✳ *SUMMARY* ✳ ✳ ✳ ✳

- Literary theory offers approaches to reading.

- Deconstruction unpacks hidden meanings through analysis of key terms in texts.

- Feminist literary criticism uncovers prejudices against women in texts, that are paraded as natural.

- Psychoanalytic literary criticism uncovers conflictual or ambivalent tensions in texts.

Where Next?

IN FRENCH

In French, the very best edition of *A la recherche du temps perdu* is edited by Jean-Yves Tadié in four volumes, published in Paris by Gallimard (Bibliothèque de la Pléiade) in 1987–89. The French publisher Folio uses this edition in paperback.

IN ENGLISH

In English, the most up to date translation is called *In Search of Lost Time*, published in six paperback volumes by Chatto & Windus, 1992, and based on the current Pléiade edition. *A la recherche* was originally translated, during Proust's lifetime, by C.K. Scott Moncrieff. The standard version for a long time was the Moncrieff translation revised by Terence Kilmartin in 1981. This was later fully revised by D.J. Enright. A completely new translation will be published by Penguin in due course (probably late 2001). It is worth knowing which translation you are reading, because the style and content have changed between early versions and the ones available now.

LITERARY CRITICISM

You might want to look at other critical writing about Proust's novel. Samuel Beckett's essay *Proust*, Malcolm Bowie's *Freud, Proust and Lacan: Theory as Fiction* and *Proust Among the Stars*, and Julia Kristeva's *Le Temps sensible*, are all expertly written modern accounts of the novel. Gilles Deleuze has written *Proust et les signes*, which, if you're interested in the uses of psychoanalysis for criticism, is wild and inspirational reading. Jean-Yves Tadié's biography *Proust* has been translated into English, and is by far the most authoritative account of Proust's life. There are many other critical essays, and an enormously long correspondence edited by Philip Kolb.

THE PROUST INDUSTRY

There has been a great deal of interest in *A la recherche* in recent years, particularly among filmmakers. In 1998, the Chilean director Raoul Ruiz released an experimental filmed interpretation of *Le temps retrouvé*. Earlier, Volker Schlöndorff filmed *Un amour de Swann*, as a period drama. Harold Pinter has written *The Proust Screenplay*. All three projects are worth trying to see or read. There is even a cartoon version of *Combray*, adapted and drawn by Stéphane Heuet (Paris: Delcourt, 1998).

You can visit Proust's holiday home in Illiers-Combray, South-West of Paris, and also see his flat in Paris at 102, boulevard Haussmann. It is currently a bank, but guided tours are still possible. The text of *A la recherche* is available online via universities using a text archiving service called FRANTEXT.

The best way forward with *A la recherche*, however, is to read it all over again.

Glossary

Allegory
Literally 'speaking otherwise'. A story with a double meaning, which operates at two or more levels.

Analogy
A likeness found between different things. A metaphor is an analogy in which the qualities of one thing are swapped for the qualities of another.

Autobiography
Literally 'self life writing'. A person's life story written by him or herself.

Biography
Literally 'life writing'. A life written by a third party.

Decadence
A literary attitude evident in nineteenth-century French symbolist poetry and literature. (see Chapter 4)

Deconstruction
A way of analysing language. Rather than seeing language as conveying fixed meanings, a deconstructionist questions whether those meanings are actually so certain.

Feminist criticism
Questions prejudices parading themselves as truths about the nature of femininity, embedded in everyday speech, political rhetoric, and action. It seeks to retrieve the work (intellectual, artistic, scientific) of women which has been lost to view or appropriated by others.

First-person voice
Writing directly about subjective, or personal, experience. Confessional narratives and autobiographies are in the first person.

Framing devices
Items such as nouns, facts, dates, times and orders of events, in sentences or whole stories, which structure them, and make them seem 'safe', i.e. credible.

Impressionism
A concerted attempt, at the end of the nineteenth century, to revise stale ways of viewing landscape and figures. It shifted emphasis from the object to the way the object was committed to canvas, thus paving the way for the art movements of the twentieth century, such as Cubism, Dadaism, Surrealism, and Expressionism.

Memory
Event in the past recalled; erratic, associative faculty which does the recalling. What we remember is what we happen not to forget.

Metaphor
Figure of speech in which one thing is described in terms of another.

Metaphysics
The study of being. The analysis of 'first principles', the real basics – time, space, causality, identity.

Modernism
In literary terms, loosely designates writers including T.S. Eliot, Pound, Joyce, Woolf, Yeats and D.H. Lawrence. Modernist writing was often informed by the works of Freud. It was characterized by thorough-going experimentation in language and form. In English modernist writing, stream of consciousness is a major technique, as is dependence upon prose, poetic imagery and myth.

Ontology
The study of being, the attempt to analyse what it means to exist at all, and how we can grasp this meaning.

Pastiche
Literary imitation which points up the comedy in what is imitated.

Post-modernism
In literary terms, a self-conscious mode of writing, which develops the lessons of modernist experimentation in form and style, and its focus on the subjective experience. Post-modern writing, by authors such as Marguerite Duras, Salman Rushdie, David Malouf, Martin Amis, or Toni Morrison, is characterized by a deliberate attempt to manipulate literary conventions.

Sources are borrowed from older works (intertextuality), and used as artificial founding myths. No allegiance is sworn to any single school or ideology.

Psychoanalysis
A therapeutic method that seeks to cure neurosis. It does so through the analysis of mental associations.

Selfhood
The way we understand ourselves as having an individual character and existence, separate from anybody else's.

Sign
A 'sign' is made up of a signifier (word) and a signified (object). These are not linked by any natural resemblance. The sign 'chair' is made up of the letters C-H-A-I-R (the signifier) together with the object it designates (a four-legged thing to sit on – the signified).

Subjectivity
Individual perspective on the world; personal preferences and desires, based on formative early influences.

Theory
Literally, a way of seeing something, a model, design, or perspective attempting to describe or control reality.

CHRONOLOGY OF MAJOR WORKS

1871 Marcel Proust born, Paris.

1895 Begins *Jean Santeuil*, unfinished novel.

1896 Publishes *Les Plaisirs et les Jours* – at his own expense. Preface by Anatole France.

1899 Abandons *Jean Santeuil*. Translates Ruskin's *The Bible of Amiens*.

1905 Writes preface to translation of Ruskin's *Sesame and Lilies*.

1907 Writes 'Sentiments filiaux d'un parricide'.

1908 Begins *Contre Sainte-Beuve*, essay of literary criticism. Develops series of pastiches of French writers, based on Lemoine fake diamonds scandal.

1909 *A la recherche du temps perdu* begins to crystallize. Originally entitled *Les Intermittences du cœur* (*The Discontinuities of the Heart*).

1912 Search for editor: Fasquelle, and Gallimard, refuse *Le Temps perdu* (*Lost Time*), first part of *Les Intermittences*. Second part, *Le Temps retrouvé* (*Time Regained*) is already in handwritten form.

1913 Publishes *Du côté de chez Swann* (*Swann's Way*), mid-November at his own expense, with Grasset. Mid-May, changes overall title to *A la recherche du temps perdu*.

1914 First World War begins. Grasset mobilized: closes publishing house.

1915 Drafting *Sodome et Gomorrhe*, *La Prisonnière*, *Albertine disparue*. Massive internal expansion to *A la recherche* throughout the First World War.

1916 Gide revises original rejection, asks Proust to publish with Gallimard/Nouvelle Revue Française.

1917 *A l'ombre des jeunes filles en fleurs* (*In the Shade of Blossoming Girls*) in proof.

1918 Essentially finishes manuscript of *A la recherche*. But revision continues.

1919   *A l'ombre des jeunes filles* published. It wins prestigious Prix
        Goncourt by a narrow majority. *Pastiches et mélanges* and
        re-edition of *Swann* published.

1920   *Le Côté de Guermantes I* (*Guermantes Way*) published.

1921   *Le Côté de Guermantes II, Sodome et Gomorrhe I* published.

1922   *Sodome et Gomorrhe II* published. *Sodome et Gomorrhe III*
        and *La Prisonnière* published. 18 November, Proust dies,
        Paris.

1925   *Albertine disparue* published.

1927   *Le Temps retrouvé* published.

1952   *Jean Santeuil* published.

1954   *Contre Sainte-Beuve* published.

INDEX